Featherstone

Susie Rosback, Natalie and
Sally Featherstone

# INSPIRING
# PLAY SPACES

Supporting creativity through
open-ended learning environments

Featherstone Education
An imprint of Bloomsbury Publishing Plc

50 Bedford Square
London
WC1B 3DP
UK

1385 Broadway
New York
NY 10018
USA

www.bloomsbury.com

Text © Susie Rosback, Natalie Coulson and Sally Featherstone, 2014
This UK edition of *Inspiring Play Spaces* is published by Bloomsbury Publishing Plc by
arrangement with Teaching Solutions, Australia
Interior photographs © Teaching Solutions, 2013, © Shutterstock
Cover photographs © London Early Years Foundation, 2014
Design by Lynda Murray, 2014

British Library Cataloguing-in-Publication Data
A catalogue record for this book is available from the British Library.

ISBN
PB 978-1-4729-1336-4
ePDF 978-1-4729-1337-1

Library of Congress Cataloging-in-Publication Data
A catalog record for this book is available from the Library of Congress.

1 3 5 7 9 10 8 6 4 2

Printed and bound in India by Replika Press Pvt. Ltd.

This book is produced using paper that is made from wood grown in managed, sustainable
forests. It is natural, renewable and recyclable. The logging and manufacturing processes
conform to the environmental regulations of the country of origin.

To view more of our titles please visit www.bloomsbury.com

## Acknowledgements

Thank you to Barney Rivers and Ruth Siems for the opportunity to write this book and share our ideas with our colleagues.

Thank you to the parents and children who inspire us every day and help us to become better practitioners.

Thank you to the wonderful colleagues we work with, who share their ideas and assist us in discovering treasures to use in our play spaces.

Thank you to Lease Cowen for creating so many of the play spaces you see in this book – you are a very creative and dedicated practitioners.

Thank you to Each Child Community Child and Family Centre in Ringwood and Brentwood Park Kindergarten in Croydon for sharing some of your inspirational play spaces.

Thank you to our families who have supported us throughout – David, Annabelle and Tom, Rhys, Thomas and Edward.

# Contents

*Daniel, Ryan and Sam enjoyed playing with the cars.*

# Preface

*Inspiring Play Spaces* was originally written in 2013 for early years practitioners in Australia, who are implementing the curriculum for early years education. The authors are both experienced kindergarten teachers who have collected photographic examples and practical ideas to illustrate the curriculum in action and, in the original edition these were linked to the Australian Early Years Framework (Being, Belonging and Becoming, 2009).

The book has now been adapted to relate to the Early Years Foundation Stage (EYFS, 2014) in England, while retaining the photos and examples of good practice from the original edition. The text has now been carefully linked to the Early Leaning Goals, highlighting the particular benefit of each area of provision. This UK edition also identifies statements from the Characteristics of Effective Learning described in Development Matters (Early Education). These statements underline the place, purpose and benefits of play materials throughout the early years and into Key Stage 1.

*Inspiring Play Spaces* is designed to encourage early years practitioners to create open-ended play spaces that will support imagination and creativity, while implementing the EYFS Framework.

## How to use this book

The book is divided into chapters, which reflect the range of experiences that practitioners provide every day. Photographs are used to demonstrate some of these experiences, with guidance on how they can be set up and enhanced, using simple, affordable materials. The authors do not intend that practitioners should read the book from cover to cover. Instead, they suggest that practitioners should dip into chapters that interest them, either because of their familiarity, or because they offer challenges in a particular setting to give a lift to the activities currently on offer.

Chapters 1–3 explore some fundamentals of the creative environment, outline a range of inspiring resources you may wish to gather for your setting, and offer some information on the stages of development in early creativity.

Chapters 4–15 take each area of provision and link it to the Early Learning Goals (ELG) and the guidance for observing the Characteristics of Effective Learning (CEL).

***Sally Featherstone***
(Based on the Preface in the original edition by Susie Rosback and Natalie Coulson.)

# Chapter 1

# Why we do what we do

When creating play spaces we focus on four features:

- play–based learning

- open-ended play spaces

- access to play equipment and

- natural and open-ended resources

These features have strong links with the Early Years Foundation Stage (EYFS) and enhance children's experiences as they play, enabling them to demonstrate the Characteristics of Effective Learning (CEL). These features are the keys to providing outstanding settings for the early years as described by OFSTED in inspection guidance.

*Using bean bags to develop throwing, balancing and catching skills.*

*Patrick, Archer and Tom made instruments and formed a band.*

## Play-based learning

The EYFS places a strong emphasis on play–based learning in the early years curriculum, stating that:

> *Each area of learning and development must be implemented through planned, purposeful play and through a mix of adult-led and child-initiated activity. Play is essential for children's development, building their confidence as they learn to explore, to think about problems, and relate to others. Children learn by leading their own play and by taking part in play which is guided by adults.*
>
> **Framework for the EYFS 2014**

*Making 'sand cakes' in the outdoor area.*

As practitioners, we know that play gives children opportunities to investigate, explore, discover, try, fail, succeed, observe, imagine, dream, pretend, share, communicate listen and participate in activities with others. Play enables children to explore who they are and who they want to become.

In the latest guidance, practitioners are encouraged to recognise the essential part they play in providing 'purposeful play', gently guiding children by playing alongside them, encouraging talk, problem solving, discussion questioning and thinking. To support this self- evaluation, the current framework has identified a range of Characteristics of Effective Learning that practitioners can use when planning, observing and interacting with the children as they play. This book will help you to recognise the value of play experiences, not just as enjoyable activities for young children, but as key places where effective learning is evident and can be observed. The key statements in each section will also enable you to evaluate and improve your setting's provision by identifying areas for development and suggesting activities that might be useful.

*Tom learnt how to hold a chicken on a farm visit.*

## Open-ended play spaces

Children will learn at their own pace if they are given the freedom to choose and engage with resources at their own level. Practitioners also know that children show what they can confidently do when they are engaged in open-ended places and with open-ended resources.

It has now been clearly stated that in open-ended activities, the adult is play-partner, enabler and co-learner, supporting and extending the child's own learning, not directing or 'teaching'. In these situations, children will produce their own creations, constructions and objects, and no two will be the same – we will no longer see 25 identical Mothers' Day cards, or worksheets completed by every child regardless of their individual abilities and interests.

The 'Enabling Environment' has been identified as a vital feature in outstanding early years settings:

> "Children learn and develop well in **enabling environments**, in which their experiences respond to their individual needs and there is a strong partnership between practitioners and parents and/or carers."
>
> **Framework for the EYFS 2014**

*George, Kaz and Jessica were inspired by the book 'Where The Wild Things Are' when creating these drawings.*

A creative learning environment is full of surprises and 'fascinations'. There is a wide range of resources available for the children to select from, plenty of space, objects, photos and paintings to inspire, and adults available to enhance the experience. Creative play is not something done 'over there' while the adults work with focus groups — it is an important and valued range of activities, accompanied by adults who are there to celebrate children's work, and encourage children and other adults to look at the processes of learning, not just the end product.

## Access to play equipment

Practitioners need to be creative too! They need to recognise a need, respond to a request and provide inspiring resources in a way that is accessible to the children. The previous practice of 'setting up' tables or other activities in a way that left no room for the children's own ideas and 'fascinations' will, at best, lead to frustration, and at worst lead to chaos as children try to find space for their own creations or activities among the resources the adults have assumed they will choose!

Good observation practices will identify the children's current interests, where additional resources might enhance or extend the play. These should be offered tactfully, in containers or in spaces where children can collect them and add them to their play if they want to.

The organisation of the setting is vital, and practitioners might usefully kneel down in their own settings, putting their eyes and ears at the level of the children, to get some idea of how they might collect the resources and play materials they need. This activity often results in a re-organisation of the space to make resources more easily accessed by the children.

Of course, in some settings, space is limited, and in these settings, photo books, wall displays, or inventive use of containers or storage units will help children to remember what is on offer.

*Grace is selecting which farm animals to use in the play corner.*

*Children can see clearly the art and craft supplies available to them and are encouraged to request items they need at any time.*

*This well–loved resource was created using sand, bark, logs and leaves.*

## Natural and open-ended resources

These resources should be in plentiful supply, as they are recognised as being extremely effective in encouraging effective learning and creative and critical thinking.

Natural products – rocks, stones and pebbles, wood shavings, shells, leaves, flowers, seeds, plants, cones, logs and branches, grasses and more – are all easily available for use indoors and outside. Adding some 'loose parts' such as glass beads, tyres and wheels, washers, nuts and bolts, and small world people and animals will enhance children's work with water, sand, mud, compost, paper shreddings, clay, dough or other malleable materials.

If you take the children on regular walks in your locality, and also encourage them to bring objects from holidays and family walks, these resources can be topped up regularly.

Offer boxes, wooden and plastic trays, mats, small pieces of carpet and pieces of fabric for children to incorporate in their play. These resources will enable children to work individually or in small groups, creating their own worlds for animals and people, and playing out situations from stories or their own lives.

In each of the chapters of the book you will find key statements from the Characteristics of Effective Learning, which you can use to evaluate your provision and assess how well you offer an enabling environment for the children.

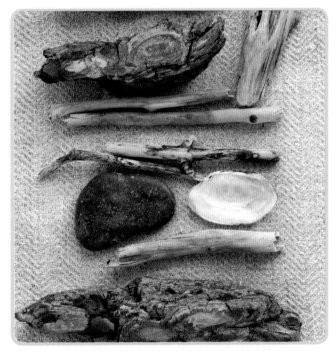

### REFLECTION

Learning in an environment that emerges from the children's interests develops a love of learning and a sense of respect, belonging and efficacy. Being able to respond to a child's interests after discussions with children is a skill all practitioners must develop in today's early childhood education culture.

# Chapter 2

# Inspiring resources

In order to run an early years setting in line with current regulatory requirements, settings should have the following resources on offer. We don't include here the obvious paper, paints, felt pens, glue, musical instruments, blocks, rolling pins, scissors, building blocks... the list could go on and on. The resources listed in this chapter are the sorts of things you will need to scrounge and forage for. They are the special treasures found in the charity or bargain shop around the corner, offcuts from your nearest fabric shop, bits and bobs from your local park or your garden, or maybe some treasures you have collected during a weekend away at the beach or in the country.

*Plants*

*Rocks*

*Logs*

*Bark and sticks*

*Herbs*

*Shells*

*Stones*

*Mini pine cones and seed pods*

*Fabric table cloths*

*Knotted logs*

*Bargain shop treasures*

*Toy animals and small world people*

*Containers and baskets*

*Assorted bowls*

# Chapter 3

# Creative development

The three main stages of artistic development observed in early childhood are 'manipulative', 'symbolic' and 'recognisable'.

## Manipulative

This refers to the stage when children are getting a feel for art by pounding, squeezing, scribbling and splatting. These are all important tasks in this stage. Children in this stage will often paint over the same spot in different colours, scribble on several pieces of paper or enjoy thumping clay but creating nothing, which is vital in a child's artistic development.

Don't try to rush this stage as it's important for the child to learn about the media they are exploring, and don't tell children they are wasting paper if they scribble on several sheets, as this is all important for creating readiness to move on to the next stage.

## Symbolic

This refers to the stage when children tell you they have painted a picture of 'Mummy' or made a dinosaur, but the art is still not recognisable to us. The child's imagination has begun to influence what they do and how they see the world. However, their art still looks like scribble or clumps of clay – although to the child it is a masterpiece.

If the child wants to tell you what they have created it is important to acknowledge their art by listening to or writing down their words, as this shows you respect their work. However, if the child is not keen to tell you what they have drawn or created then don't ask, as often it is just exploration of the pen and paper, not a drawing of anything. If a child feels they must always draw 'something' they may not want to draw at all. Using praise such as 'I love your use of colour', 'I love the way you have covered the page' or 'It looks as if you enjoyed creating that masterpiece', show the child that you respect their work but they don't have to 'produce' for you to make you happy. Educating families and helping them understand this information may lead to children feeling more able, enthusiastic and adventurous with their creativity.

*Axel painted a tornado.*

# Recognisable

In this stage of artistic development, a child will create things that are recognisable to others. A person will resemble a person. Children will begin drawing flowers, trees, animals and many other items and you will begin to recognise what these are without having to ask. As the child develops, more detail will be added.

The child's power of observation is developing at this stage and, as time passes, they will become bolder and more adventurous with what they are willing to try. The pictures below show more detail appearing in drawings as the children have practised and refined their skills.

Eventually children will be painting/drawing scenes with great detail and skill.

*In this picture, a pterodactyl is flying towards a volcano and it has started to rain (by Sienna).*

# A few do's and don'ts

## DON'T ...

- suggest the child fills the page

- restrict the amount of paper being used

- try to hurry a child through the stages of creative development

- use broken or poor quality art materials

- ask for explanations of the child's unrecognisable work – if there is a meaning you will learn it. If recognisable, you can say 'tell me more about this.'

## DO...

- talk to the children about the shapes they have used to create certain things

- look at other children's work and discuss their art and what they have created to stimulate children's thinking. This follows Vygotsky's theory that children learn from others with greater knowledge and skill than themselves

- display children's work for all to see – this way, the children will realise how important their contributions are

- encourage the children and show respect for their creations

- educate families to understand these stages of artistic development and not to send children off demanding they paint or draw for them today

- offer the best quality art supplies your setting can afford. Better quality art materials stimulate creativity, support exploration and discovery and encourage children to have a go

- take the drawing materials to children in their chosen areas, rather than expecting them to always come to a drawing table or easel.

# Chapter 4

# Manipulative play experiences

Manipulative experiences should be designed in a way that will spark creativity, be inviting and support children's learning. Each day it is likely that one or other of these experiences will be offered to the children in your setting.

Manipulative activities have numerous developmental benefits that support early learning outcomes. With a little inspiration, your play dough table can become a place of wonder and imagination, and will soon be surrounded by children and adults inspired to create, explore and discover.

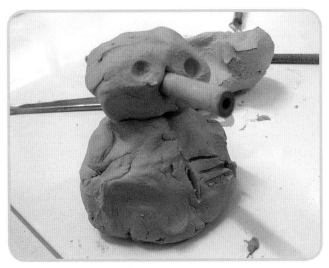

*This snowman was created with clay and a wooden tube.*

*Using items from your storage cupboard, such as gemstones, rocks and toy animals, makes play dough more inviting.*

*Zara shows that she is happy and satisfied with her ice-cream creation!*

# Early Learning Goals from the EYFS

Playing with manipulative materials enables children to work towards the following Early Learning Goals. Key features of these that relate to manipulative play are identified in *italics*:

## Personal, social and emotional development

Making relationships:

*Children play co-operatively, taking turns with others. They take account of one another's ideas about how to organise their activity.* They show sensitivity to others' needs and feelings, and form positive relationships with adults and other children.

## Physical development

Moving and handling:

*Children show good control and co-ordination in large and small movements.* They move confidently in a range of ways, safely negotiating space. They handle equipment and tools effectively, including pencils for writing.

## Expressive arts and design

Exploring and using media and materials:

Children sing songs, make music and dance, and experiment with ways of changing them. *They safely use and explore a variety of materials, tools and techniques*, experimenting with colour, design, texture, form and function.

Being imaginative:

*Children use what they have learnt about media and materials in original ways, thinking about uses and purposes. They represent their own ideas, thoughts and feelings* through design and technology, art, music, dance, role-play and stories.

*Children who have trouble settling will often be comforted when playing with play dough.*

## Understanding the world

People and communities:

*Children talk about past and present events in their own lives and in the lives of family members.* They know that other children don't always enjoy the same things, and are sensitive to this. They know about similarities and differences between themselves and others, and among families, communities and traditions.

*Feathers and gemstones enhance the experience and end product when working with play dough, and add another tactile dimension.*

# Characteristics of Effective Learning

When children are learning through play with manipulative materials, adults will be able to observe some of the Characteristics of Effective Learning from the EYFS. In this section, the photos are accompanied by some of these 'CEL' statements:

*(Note: In the following text, P&E = Playing and Exploring; AL = Active Learning; CTC= Creating and Thinking Critically)*

## The unique child

(Observing how a child is learning)

Children may:

- Use their senses to explore the world around them. P&E2

- Engage in open-ended activity. P&E3

- Pretend objects are things from their experience. P&E5

- Represent their experiences in play. P&E6

- Initiate activities. P&E9

- Show a 'can do' attitude. P&E11

- Maintain focus on their activity for a period of time. AL1

- Show high levels of energy, fascination. AL2

- Persisting with activity when challenges occur. AL5

- Show satisfaction in meeting their own goals. AL8

- Be proud of how they accomplished something – not just the end result. AL9

- Test their ideas. CTC6

- Plan, make decisions about how to approach a task, solve a problem and reach a goal. CTC8

*Children were required to apply thinking strategies to solve the problem of creating a bus for the bears.*

## Positive relationships

(What adults could do)

Adults may:

- Play with children. Encourage them to explore, and showing their own interest in discovering new things. P&E1

- Join in play sensitively, fit in with children's ideas. P&E3

- Model pretending an object is something else, and help develop roles and stories. P&E4

- Pay attention to how children engage in activities – the challenges faced, the effort, thought, learning and enjoyment. Talk more about the process than products. P&E6

- Support children to choose their activities – what they want to do and how they will do it. AL1

- Describe what they see children trying to do, and encourage them to talk about their own processes and successes. AL3

- Encourage open-ended thinking by not settling on the first ideas: *What else is possible*? CTC3

- Always respect children's efforts and ideas, so they feel safe to take a risk with a new idea. CTC4

- Talk aloud to help children to think about and control what they do. Adults may be modeling self-talk, describing their actions in play. CTC5

- Give children time to talk and think. CTC6

- Follow children's lead in conversation, and think about things together. Sustained shared thinking helps children to explore ideas and make links. CTC10

## Enabling environments
(What adults could provide)

Adults could provide additional support by:

- Providing stimulating resources which are accessible and open-ended so they can be used, moved and combined in a variety of ways. P&E1

- Planning first-hand experiences and challenges appropriate to the development of the children. P&E5

- Ensuring children have uninterrupted time to play and explore. P&E6

- Providing something that is new and unusual for them to explore, especially when it is linked to their interests. AL1

- Keeping significant activities out instead of routinely tidying them away. AL5

- Asking themselves: *Is this an opportunity for children to find their own ways to represent and develop their own ideas?* Avoid children just reproducing someone else's ideas. CTC1

- Building in opportunities for children to play with materials before using them in planned tasks. CTC2

- Establishing the enabling conditions for rich play: space, time, flexible resources, choice, control, warm and supportive relationships Play is a key opportunity for children to think creatively and flexibly, solve problems and link ideas. CTC3

- Developing a learning community which focuses on how and not just what we are learning. CTC8

*After some of the children had shown an interest in dinosaurs they created dinosaurs from clay.*

*A lovely flower garden was made using play dough, flowers and wooden sticks.*

*Tom used the play dough to create his own name – a wonderful way of supporting his identity while developing his understanding of literacy and text.*

# RECIPES

The activities on the next few pages all revolve around the use of these malleable materials.

## No-cook play dough recipe

Because this is made with boiled water it is **only suitable for adults to make.**

*2 cups plain flour*

*1 cup salt*

*4 tablespoons cream of tartar*

*1 tablespoon cooking oil*

*1–1½ cups boiled water*

*(optional — natural food colouring, few drops essential oil, rice for texture)*

1.  Put all the dry ingredients together in a bowl.

2.  Make a well and put in the oil (if you are adding colour, mix the food colouring with the oil).

3.  Add the boiling water from the kettle and mix it all together. Give it a few minutes to cool down before kneading. Keep it in a container.

## Alternative no-cook play dough

*2 cups plain flour*

*1 cup of salt*

*1 tbs oil (or a little more if you want)*

*1 cup of cold water*

*2 drops of food colouring*

1.  Mix together and play!

## Salt dough

Salt dough is a wonderful product that is used to create crafts, sculptures and ornaments. It can be easily made at home using 3 basic ingredients and then placed in the oven to dry out.

*1 cup salt*

*2 cups of flour*

*¾ cup of water*

1.  In a large bowl, mix the salt and flour together.

2.  Gradually stir in the water. Mix well until it forms a doughy consistency.

3.  Turn the dough onto the bench and knead with your hands until smooth and combined.

4.  Make your creations using the salt dough.

Place the salt dough creations into the oven at 180°C. The amount of time needed to bake depends on the size and thickness of the salt dough creations.

### TIPS AND IDEAS:

✓ Store your salt dough in an airtight container as it keeps fresh for a few days.

✓ You can paint your creations with acrylic paints and seal with varnish or polyurethane spray.

✓ Salt dough can also be aired dried and is an alternative to oven drying.

✓ Involve the kids in making the salt dough as this encourages and promotes so many learning opportunities, plus it is lots of fun!

# Dinosaur play dough

Dinosaur inspired play dough with pebbles, trees, rolling pins and occasionally two colours of dough.

**3** ...And by day three, the dough was all orange.

**1** On day one, the children were offered two colours of dough to work with.

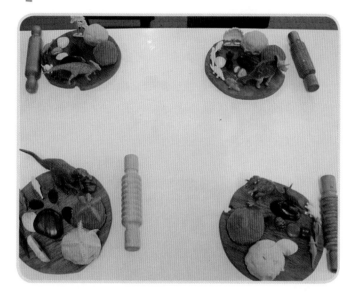

**4** With a slight change of the display and an addition of more of the pink dough, the activity was made fresh and inviting the next day.

**2** On day two, the colours had mixed to create a marbling effect.

**5** Using fresh branches from the garden and old bones (thoroughly cleaned) adds interest to the play experience and strengthens the theme.

## Cake shop

The cake shop is a similar experience. An old tiered cake tray, some china plates, play dough cakes from the home corner and rolling pins displayed in a tin bucket help make an inviting place to play.

## Natural products

The use of natural products such as shells, lavender, rosemary, sand, pebbles and leaves brings the play dough to life, adds aromas and textures and makes the experience more appealing. Items such as fabric, starfish, artificial grass, plastic animals and interesting baskets and bowls help in the final presentation.

## Black play dough

To make your own fossils, add black food colouring to the dough and provide plastic bugs, spiders and beetles for children to choose from. For another idea, provide goggle eyes, pipe cleaners, lolly sticks, gemstones and more to allow children to create their own bugs and spiders.

## Chocolate play dough

Using chocolate extract and brown food colouring you can create delicious smelling chocolate play dough. Add a tablespoon of cocoa powder to really stimulate the senses. The children can make chocolates or little chocolate cakes – but remind them that the dough is not edible. The addition of old chocolate boxes, gemstones, glitter and other decorative items make this a lovely 'cooking' experience.

*Staff supported children's interest in cooking by helping them make chocolate play dough.*

## Salt dough decorations

Take children on a nature walk to find textured natural objects such as pine cones, berries and leaves. Back in the setting, use cookie cutters to stamp shapes out of the salt dough, then encourage children to choose a natural item to press onto the raw dough to create a wonderful imprint. Try theming this idea according to the time of year: at Christmas, for instance, collect your objects on a winter walk, then use cookie cutter shapes such as Christmas trees, reindeer and stars. Using a drinking straw, make a hole in the top of the decoration, bake, and finally thread a ribbon through each decoration so children can hang them on a tree.

## Bakery

Add wholemeal flour to the play dough to make it look like bread dough. Provide chopping boards, rolling pins, little bread tins and also some poppy seeds and other seeds to decorate the 'bread'. A chalk board is a great touch, displaying today's bakery specials.

## Clay

When first introducing clay it is a good idea to keep it simple while the children explore the texture and get a feel for the new medium. Later providing wooden beads, pinecones, clay tools, garlic crushers, leaves, pebbles and more will make the clay a great source of interest. Set mirrors up opposite the play space to encourage children to observe their movements.

## Stimulate the senses

Other things to add that will stimulate the senses at the play dough table are lavender oil, rosemary and fresh lavender. At Easter time, add spices and cinnamon to give that delightful aroma of hot-cross buns.

At Halloween, try making mini pumpkins by using orange play dough and adding spices such as ginger, nutmeg, cinnamon, whole cloves and star anise for decoration. Provide green pipe cleaners or the lids from green marker pens in case the children want to add 'stalks'.

Presenting the play dough or clay in different shapes also makes it more appealing to look at and can encourage children to think of new ways of playing with the material. You can add glitter, rice, beads, stones, seeds, feathers and so on to the play dough to add texture.

# Chapter 5

# Drawing

If drawing experiences are set up in a manner that is visually appealing, organised and stimulating then the children are more likely to be creative and enthusiastic about the masterpieces they create. Drawing is an experience that can be offered at all times in an early years setting.

To support children in their artistic development, it is vital they have plenty of opportunity to explore different drawing media at their own level and pace. (For more detail on creative development, refer to Chapter 3.) There are a multitude of other developmental benefits such as fine motor development, eye–hand coordination and language development, to name but a few.

*Dividing the colours into separate colour–coded containers helps children to develop sorting and categorising skills.*

## Early learning outcomes

Drawing experiences support many learning outcomes by encouraging children to:

- be open to new challenges, make new discoveries and feel recognised and respected.

- explore connections, similarities and differences between people.

- share fun, happiness and satisfaction.

- celebrate their own and others' efforts and achievements, make choices and take appropriate risks.

- become curious and enthusiastic participants in their own learning.

- persevere and experience the satisfaction of achievement.

- use literacy and mathematics in role-play, using and enjoying language, mark making and text in a range of ways.

These are just some of the ways in which drawing experiences support children's learning and development.

# Early Learning Goals from the EYFS

Drawing and mark making enable children to work towards the following Early Learning Goals. Key features of these that relate to drawing are identified in *italics*:

## Personal, social and emotional development

Making relationships:

*Children play co-operatively, taking turns with others. They take account of one another's ideas about how to organise their activity.* They show sensitivity to others' needs and feelings, and form positive relationships with adults and other children.

Self-confidence and self-awareness:

*Children are confident to try new activities, and say why they like some activities more than others.* They are confident to speak in a familiar group, will talk about their ideas, and will *choose the resources they need for their chosen activities. They say when they do or don't need help.*

## Physical development

Moving and handling:

*Children show good control and co-ordination in large and small movements.* They move confidently in a range of ways, safely negotiating space. *They handle equipment and tools effectively, including pencils for writing.*

*Try encouraging children to draw using fine liner pens then paint their drawings.*

*Providing drawing experiences outside allows children to develop skills in a different setting.*

## Mathematics

Shape, space and measures:

Children use everyday language to talk about size, weight, capacity, position, distance, time and money to compare quantities and objects and to solve problems. *They recognise, create and describe patterns. They explore characteristics of everyday objects and shapes and use mathematical language to describe them.*

## Understanding the world

The world:

Children know about similarities and differences in relation to places, objects, materials and living things. They talk about the features of their own immediate environment and how environments might vary from one another. They make observations about animals and plants and explain why some things occur, and talk about changes.

Technology:

Children recognise that a range of technology is used in places such as homes and schools. *They select and use technology for particular purposes.*

## Expressive arts and design

Exploring and using media and materials:

Children sing songs, make music and dance, and experiment with ways of changing them. They safely use and explore a variety of materials, tools and techniques, experimenting with colour, design, texture, form and function.

Being imaginative:

Children use what they have learnt about media and materials in original ways, thinking about uses and purposes. They represent their own ideas, thoughts and feelings through design and technology, art, music, dance, role-play and stories.

# Characteristics of Effective Learning

When children are learning through drawing and mark making, adults will be able to observe some of the Characteristics of Effective Learning from the EYFS. In this section, the photos are accompanied by some of these 'CEL' statements:

*(Note: In the following text, P&E = Playing and Exploring; AL = Active Learning; CTC= Creating and Thinking Critically)*

## The unique child
(Observing how a child is learning)

Children may:

- Show curiosity about objects, events and people. P&E1

- Use senses to explore the world around them. P&E2

- Engage in open-ended activity. P&E3

- Show particular interests. P&E4

- Represent their experiences in play. P&E6

- Initiate activities. P&E9

- Seek challenge. P&E10

- Show a 'can do' attitude. P&E11

- Take a risk, engaging in new experiences, and learning by trial and error. P&E12

- Maintain focus on their activity for a period of time. AL1

- Show high levels of energy, fascination. AL2

- Be not easily distracted. AL3

- Pay attention to details. AL4

- Persist with activity when challenges occur. AL5

- Show satisfaction in meeting their own goals. AL8

- Be proud of how they accomplished something – not just the end result. AL9

- Think of ideas. CTC1

## Positive relationships
(What adults could do)

Adults may:

- Help children as needed to do what they are trying to do, without taking over or directing. P&E2

- Encourage children to try new activities and to judge risks for themselves. Be sure to support children's confidence with words and body language. P&E5

- Talk about how you and the children get better at things through effort and practice, and what we all can learn when things go wrong. P&E7

- Support children to choose their activities – what they want to do and how they will do it. AL1

- Describe what they see children trying to do, and encourage children to talk about their own processes and successes. AL3

- Be specific when praising, especially noting effort such as how the child concentrates, tries different approaches, persists, solves problems, and has new ideas. AL4

- Encourage children to learn together, and from each other. AL5

- Help children to develop their own motivations by giving reasons and talking about learning, rather than just directing. AL6

- Always respect children's efforts and ideas, so they feel safe to take a risk with a new idea. CTC4

- Give children time to talk and think. CTC6

- Support children's interests over time, reminding them of previous approaches and encouraging them to make connections between their experiences. CTC8

- Give feedback and help children to review their own progress and learning. Talk with children about what they are doing, how they plan to do it, what worked well and what they would change next time. CTC13

*While drawing their self-portraits, children talked about the features of their faces and bodies.*

## Enabling environment

(What adults could provide)

Adults could provide additional support by:

- Offering stimulating resources which are accessible and open-ended so they can be used, moved and combined in a variety of ways. P&E1

- Making sure resources are relevant to children's interests. P&E2

- Arranging flexible indoor and outdoor space and resources where children can explore, build, move and role-play. P&E3

- Helping children to concentrate by limiting noise and making spaces visually calm and orderly. P&E4

- Noticing what arouses children's curiosity, looking for signs of deep involvement to identify learning that is intrinsically motivated. AL2

- Ensuring children have time and freedom to become deeply involved in activities. AL3

- Children can maintain focus on things that interest them over a period of time. Adults can help children to keep ideas in mind by talking over photographs of their previous activities. AL4

- Keeping significant activities out instead of routinely tidying them away. AL5

- In planning activities, adults could ask themselves: *Is this an opportunity for children to find their own ways to represent and develop their own ideas?* Avoid children just reproducing someone else's ideas. CTC1

- Use mind-maps to represent thinking together. CTC7

- Develop a learning community which focuses on how and not just what we are learning. CTC8

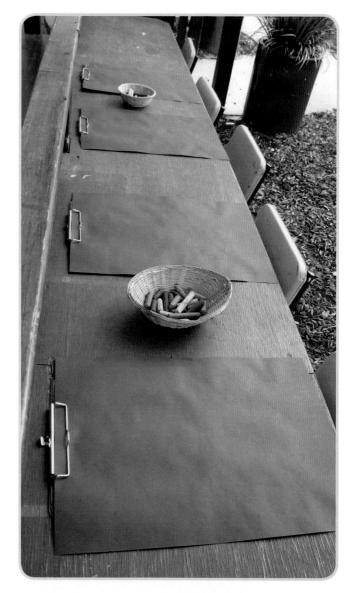

*Putting drawing materials outside broadens opportunities for developing creativity.*

Drawing can be done:

✓ on wood, sandpaper, tracing paper, aluminium foil, paper plates, corrugated cardboard, newspaper, coloured paper, plain paper

✓ using crayons, charcoal, felt tip pens, pastels, pencils, chalk, fine line black pens

✓ observing dinosaurs, bugs, zoo animals, flowers, trucks and more on a drawing table

✓ while standing up at an easel, sitting down at a table, lying on the floor, at a chalkboard, listening to music, outdoors, using clipboards – in whatever environment children feel most comfortable

## Drawing tables

Creating an organised; visually pleasing drawing table will attract children to using it. Dividing colours into separate containers develops children's ability to sort and categorise, simplifies the choices for children and is organised and inviting. As children get older, providing several different types of drawing media can assist in making choices and developing organisational skills.

Providing access to the alphabet, envelopes, photos and a container of words will encourage children to have a go at writing when they are ready. Placemats define the space for each child and make the environment look more appealing. Covering the table with paper or a table cloth also looks great. Displaying photos of the children with their names underneath will encourage children to write to each other.

Placing black paper and white pens near a light table/board encourages children to have a go at drawing skeletons. You could also add a model 3D skeleton to the table so they can observe the detail more closely.

## Visual stimulation

Adding toy or small world animals stimulates the children to think about drawing them. The image on the left shows how African animals were added to the drawing table after a visit to the zoo.

Dinosaurs are another a popular item to add to your tables. When adding them to the drawing table you could then sit with the children and discuss the shapes of their bodies, head and legs, and describe some features, such as the spikes on the stegosaurus. These conversations break the animal down into manageable parts that the children feel they can draw.

Each child will interpret the anima they are studying in their own way. Make sure to praise all efforts.

Bugs, spiders and beetles are an easy thing to start drawing. They are a great stimulus for younger children as they consist mainly of circles, ovals and lines.

An unused fish tank can be a great space to add a scene. In the image above, staff created a polar bear ice land using cotton balls, polystyrene, blue gemstones and plastic polar bears. Alternatively you could create an ocean tank with whales, sand, shells, seaweed and various sea creatures.

Using a bird's nest found by a child, together with some decorative birds from a charity shop and feathers from the craft cupboard is a great way to encourage children to draw something new —and the child who brought in the bird's nest will know that his ideas are valued.

## Providing variety

It is important to offer a variety of different types of drawing tools to children during their time with you. The most important point is to offer good quality drawing tools that are in good working order.

Felt–tip pens, soft pastels, oil pastels, pencils, crayons, charcoal, water colour pencils, felt tip pens, black fine line pens, white ball point pens, chalk and more will all stimulate children and encourage them to participate in the experience. Changing the art materials on a regular basis will also help to stimulate creativity.

Drawing is not limited to the indoors; it can be done wherever the child feels comfortable. Providing clipboards outdoors allows children to draw outside: the clipboards stop paper from flying away and mean that drawing can be carried to any area of the setting. Taking clipboards on excursions is a great way for children to draw things of interest when out and about.

Some children are reluctant to draw at all. This could be for any one of many reasons: perhaps they were encouraged while too young and not developmentally ready, or maybe they lack confidence. Putting clipboards and drawing materials into your home corner or at a construction table means that even a reluctant drawer will have a go when they are ready.

# Chapter 6

# Drama and role-play

Young children love to pretend. Using our imagination and role-playing are vital ingredients for developing happy, healthy children.

Some sort of dramatic play area should be available for children in your setting at all times. In fact, it would not be uncommon to have more than one role-play area available at a time. Dramatic play supports children's wellbeing, sense of belonging, language skills and social development. It also supports emotions and allows children to practise life skills.

*A huge box of dressing-up clothes can open up a number of wonderful role-play experiences.*

*Working together to sort out the roles children will take on supports a sense of identity and team work.*

# Early Learning Goals from the EYFS

Drama and role-play enable children to work towards the following Early Learning Goals. Key features of these that relate to drama and role-play are identified in *italics*:

## Personal, social and emotional development

Making relationships:

*Children play co-operatively, taking turns with others. They take account of one another's ideas about how to organise their activity.* They show sensitivity to others' needs and feelings, and form positive relationships with adults and other children.

Self-confidence and self-awareness:

Children are confident to try new activities, and say why they like some activities more than others. *They are confident to speak in a familiar group, will talk about their ideas, and will choose the resources they need for their chosen activities.* They say when they do or don't need help.

Managing feelings and behaviour:

*Children talk about how they and others show feelings, talk about their own and others' behaviour, and its consequences, and know that some behaviour is unacceptable. They work as part of a group or class, and understand and follow the rules.* They adjust their behaviour to different situations, and take changes of routine in their stride.

*Kaylee decided to be a mother, Cooper chose to pay the daddy. This play experience allowed these children to role-play a situation which provided opportunities to support each other's emotions.*

## Communication and language

Listening and attention:

*Children listen attentively in a range of situations. They listen to stories, accurately anticipating key events and respond to what they hear with relevant comments, questions or actions.* They give their attention to what others say and respond appropriately, while engaged in another activity.

Understanding:

Children follow instructions involving several ideas or actions. *They answer 'how' and 'why' questions about their experiences and in response to stories or events.*

Speaking:

*Children express themselves effectively, showing awareness of listeners' needs. They use past, present and future forms accurately when talking about events that have happened or are to happen in the future. They develop their own narratives and explanations by connecting ideas or events.*

## Physical development

Moving and handling:

Children show good control and co-ordination in large and small movements. They move confidently in a range of ways, safely negotiating space. *They handle equipment and tools effectively, including pencils for writing.*

## Understanding the world

People and communities:

*Children talk about past and present events in their own lives and in the lives of family members.* They know that other children don't always enjoy the same things, and are sensitive to this. They know about similarities and differences between themselves and others, and among families, communities and traditions.

## Technology

Children recognise that a range of technology is used in places such as homes and schools. *They select and use technology for particular purposes.*

## Expressive arts and design

Being imaginative:

Children use what they have learnt about media and materials in original ways, thinking about uses and purposes. *They represent their own ideas, thoughts and feelings through* design and technology, art, music, dance, *role-play and stories*.

# Characteristics of Effective Learning

When children are learning through role-play and drama, adults will be able to observe some of the Characteristics of Effective Learning from the EYFS. In this section, the photos are accompanied by some of these 'CEL' statements:

*(Note: In the following text, P&E = Playing and Exploring; AL = Active Learning; CTC= Creating and Thinking Critically)*

## The unique child

(Observing how a child is learning)

Children may:

- Show curiosity about objects, events and people. P&E1

- Use senses to explore the world around them. P&E2

- Engage in open-ended activity. P&E3

- Show particular interests. P&E4

- Pretend objects are things from their experience. P&E5

- Represent their experiences in play. P&E6

- Take on a role in their play. P&E7

- Act out experiences with other people. P&E8

- Initiate activities. P&E9

- Maintain focus on their activity for a period of time. AL1

- Show high levels of energy, fascination. AL2

- Make links and noticing patterns in their experience. CTC4

- Plan, make decisions about how to approach a task, solve a problem and reach a goal. CTC8

*Providing open-ended creative opportunities and resources allows children to express themselves in their own way.*

## Positive relationships

(What adults could do)

Adults may:

- Play with children. Encourage them to explore, and showing their own interest in discovering new things. P&E1

- Help children as needed to do what they are trying to do, without taking over or directing. P&E2

- Join in play sensitively, fitting in with children's ideas. P&E3

- Model pretending an object is something else, and help develop roles and stories. P&E4

- Support children to choose their activities – what they want to do and how they will do it. AL1

- Stimulate children's interest through shared attention, and calm over-stimulated children. AL2

- Encourage children to learn together, and from each other. AL5

- Use the language of thinking and learning: think, know, remember, forget, idea, makes sense, plan, learn, find out, confused, figure out, trying to do. CTC1

- Always respect children's efforts and ideas, so they feel safe to take a risk with a new idea. CTC4

- Talking aloud helps children to think and control what they do. Adults should model self-talk, describing their actions in play. CTC5

- Sustained shared thinking helps children to explore ideas and make links. Follow children's lead in conversation, and think about things together. CTC10

- Give feedback and help children to review their own progress and learning. Talk with children about what they are doing, how they plan to do it, what worked well and what they would change next time. CTC13

## Enabling environments

(What adults could provide)

Adults could provide additional support by:

- Providing stimulating resources which are accessible and open-ended so they can be used, moved and combined in a variety of ways. P&E1

- Making sure resources are relevant to children's interests. P&E2

- Arranging flexible indoor and outdoor space and resources where children can explore, build, move and role-play. P&E3

- Children will become more deeply involved when adults provide something that is new and unusual for them to explore, especially when it is linked to their interests. AL1

- Keeping significant activities out instead of routinely tidying them away. AL5

- Building in opportunities for children to play with materials before using them in planned tasks. CTC2

- Play is a key opportunity for children to think creatively and flexibly, solve problems and link ideas. Adults can promote the enabling conditions for rich play: space, time, flexible resources, choice, control, warm and supportive relationships. CTC3

- Plan linked experiences that follow the ideas children are really thinking about. CTC6

- Develop a learning community which focuses on how and not just what we are learning. CTC8

*Allowing children to be themselves is vital in supporting identity and building trusting relationships.*

# Drama

Many of the traditional nursery rhymes and stories we remember from childhood are a wonderful source of inspiration when doing drama with the children. Stories such as:

* **Goldilocks and The Three Bears**

* **The Enormous Turnip**

* **Rapunzel**

* **Three Billy Goats Gruff**

* **Jack and The Beanstalk**

all lend themselves to re-enactment and improvisation.

## Creative dance and music

Offering the children the opportunity to use their imagination to disappear into another world, do things they can only dream of and develop creativity without boundaries provides an invaluable experience.

## The home corner

The home corner should feel exactly like that – 'home'. Therefore including homely furniture, real food items that can be used throughout the year when cooking, plants, fresh flowers and crockery, just like at home, teaches the children to respect their environment and to be careful when playing.

An old vacuum cleaner or other cleaning equipment, felted food items, and any out of date spices, grains and pulses from home (with the lids taped) all add to the overall effect of creating an inviting home corner.

For younger children, the same effect can be achieved using plastic jars and crockery, if you are concerned for the children's safety. Glue the lids on to avoid having to clean up spilled contents.

## A hospital or vet corner

Doctors and nurses uniforms, a telephone, computer, waiting room, gowns, hats, breathing masks, plastic syringes and stethoscopes are all wonderful props used to create a hospital corner. This might be created in response to a child or family member needing to go to hospital, or out of natural childhood curiosity.

The addition of some animals – not real ones like Lola here – but toy animals can turn your hospital corner into a vet surgery. Lola was part of our Dog Awareness and Safety Around Animals programme. The children pictured patting Lola were terrified of dogs when we started the programme.

Please note: We do not recommend taking just any dog into an early childhood setting.

## A dressing up area

Providing a dressing-up area can allow children to express themselves in different ways. Role-playing and taking on a different persona can help quieter children feel more confident.

## A restaurant

With the addition of lanterns, chef's hats, traditional silk clothing, a phone, menus from a local Chinese restaurant, noodle boxes, chop sticks, Asian style crockery and more, we decided to transform our home corner into an Asian restaurant. In addition to offering the play area you might like to invite some adults to your setting to cook food for the children (being aware of allergies).

You could also involve family members in reading well-known children's stories in their home language and assisting you with learning greetings and important words you might use to support the children in your setting.

Of course, this concept can be used with any culture, not just Asian cultures, and it is vital to support all cultures in your setting throughout the year with similar concepts.

## An autumn corner

Do you remember what a fabulous feeling it was kicking through autumn leaves as a child? Well, in your autumn corner the children can re-create that experience. It is a great place to relax with a friend or just lie down and think about things. Using netting, separate off a corner of your room and fill it with hundreds of dry autumn leaves. This will create hours of good old-fashioned noisy fun.

A fun excursion could be taking the children on an autumn walk to gather leaves from your local area. Also, asking families to bring in bags of dry leaves will cut down the work you have in gathering leaves for your autumn corner.

Once you have finished using the leaves, families are often happy to take the leaves away as mulch for their gardens. Alternatively, if you have a compost bin, the children will enjoy helping you to add the leaves to make compost.

## A space corner

Many children are interested in space, so creating a space corner will support these children in their learning and sense of belonging. Building a rocket from a fridge box or making space outfits from items collected from your local charity shop is lots of fun.

Creating the control panel for the space station out of recycled computer parts was a sensational way to build on learning about space travel.

*This space tent was made out of black plastic. The glow-painted artifacts were illuminated by a 'blacklight'.*

## Outdoors

Creating little spaces for children to disappear into and hide with a friend is really important.

Outdoor puppet shows can be a great source of fun, which can then be extended into creating your own puppets as a craft activity. Now you know what to do with all those old socks!

## A camping area

Using an old tent – or just some fabric – you can create an inviting camping area. Add a pretend fire, a kettle for tea and some sleeping bags and cosy cushions.

## A hairdressing salon

A hairdressing salon can be created with lots of intriguing items from your local charity shop or pound shop. Try collecting sparkly containers, hair brushes, old sunglasses, empty face-cream jars, spray bottles, hair dryers (cord cut off), rollers, headbands, necklaces, eye masks and more ...

# Chapter 7

# Themed play spaces

Themed play spaces should be designed to support children playing alone, as well as together in groups of two or more. Individual play spaces support each child's need for solitary play and quiet time throughout the day. Aim to have a minimum of two of these in your setting. Being in these quiet individual places gives children unique opportunities to develop in ways that more active and busy places do not.

Many of the experiences we offer children in early childhood, however, such as construction, painting and printing, are for two or more children to enjoy at once. For open-ended, play-based experiences, incorporate nature and beautiful treasures sourced from charity shops, pound shops and, in many cases, the garden or local area.

It is important to distinguish between play spaces meant for one, and spaces meant for social interactions between children where conversations will inspire learning opportunities in small groups.

## Early Learning Goals from the EYFS

**Playing in individual play spaces** enables children to work towards the following EarlyLearning Goals, and to engage in solitary play if they so wish. Key features of these that relate to individual and group themed play spaces are identified in *italics*:

### Personal, social and emotional development

Self-confidence and self-awareness:

*Children are confident to try new activities, and say why they like some activities more than others.* They are confident to speak in a familiar group, will talk about their ideas, and will choose the resources they need for their chosen activities. *They say when they do or don't need help.*

### Communication and language

Understanding:

Children follow instructions involving several ideas or actions. *They answer 'how' and 'why' questions about their experiences and in response to stories or events.*

Speaking:

Children express themselves effectively, showing awareness of listeners' needs. *They use past, present and future forms accurately when talking about events that have happened or are to happen in the future. They develop their own narratives and explanations by connecting ideas or events.*

### Physical development

Moving and handling:

*Children show good control and co-ordination in large and small movements.* They move confidently in a range of ways, safely negotiating space. They handle equipment and tools effectively, including pencils for writing.

## Understanding the world

**People and communities:**

*Children talk about past and present events in their own lives and in the lives of family members. They know that other children don't always enjoy the same things, and are sensitive to this.* They know about similarities and differences between themselves and others, and among families, communities and traditions.

**The world:**

Children know about similarities and differences in relation to places, objects, materials and living things. *They talk about the features of their own immediate environment and how environments might vary from one another. They make observations of animals and plants and explain why some things occur, and talk about changes.*

*Open-ended play areas encourage children to make choices and show independence.*

## Expressive arts and design

**Exploring and using media and materials:**

Children sing songs, make music and dance, and experiment with ways of changing them. *They safely use and explore a variety of materials, tools and techniques, experimenting with colour, design, texture, form and function.*

**Being imaginative:**

Children use what they have learnt about media and materials in original ways, thinking about uses and purposes. *They represent their own ideas, thoughts and feelings* through design and technology, art, music, dance, role-play and stories.

# Characteristics of Effective Learning

Providing opportunities to work in quiet individual spaces offers supports independent learning and confidence in working alone, while spaces for social interaction support communication and group learning. These are some of the Characteristics of Effective Learning (EYFS) that adults may see when children are learning in themed play spaces:

*(Note: P&E = Playing and Exploring; AL = Active Learning; CTC= Creating and Thinking Critically)*

## The unique child

(observing how a child is learning)

Children may:

- Show curiosity about objects, events and people. P&E1

- Engage in open-ended activity. P&E3

- Seek challenge. P&E10

- Show a 'can do' attitude. P&E11

- Maintain focus on their activity for a period of time. AL1

- Show high levels of energy, fascination. AL2

- Be not easily distracted. AL3

- Pay attention to details. AL4

- Persist with activity when challenges occur. AL5

- Bounce back after difficulties. AL7

- Show satisfaction in meeting their own goals. AL8

- Be proud of how they accomplished something – not just the end result. AL9

- Enjoy meeting challenges for their own sake rather than external rewards or praise. AL10

- Think of ideas. CTC1

- Make links and notice patterns in their experience. CTC4

- Plan, make decisions about how to approach a task, solve a problem and reach a goal. CTC8

- Change strategy as needed. CTC10

*Plants help to make a play area inviting for children.*

## Positive relationships

(What adults could do)

Adults may:

- Help children as needed to do what they are trying to do, without taking over or directing. P&E2

- Encourage children to try new activities and to judge risks for themselves. Be sure to support children's confidence with words and body language. P&E5

- Pay attention to how children engage in activities - the challenges faced, the effort, thought, learning and enjoyment. Talk more about the process than products. P&E6

- Support children to choose their activities – what they want to do and how they will do it. AL1

- Help children to become aware of their own goals, make plans, and review their own progress and successes. AL3

- Be specific when praising, especially noting effort such as how the child concentrates, tries different approaches, persists, solves problems, and has new ideas. AL4

- Encourage open-ended thinking by not settling on the first ideas: What else is possible? CTC3

- Always respecting children's efforts and ideas, so they feel safe to take a risk with a new idea. CTC4

- Give children time to talk and think. CTC6

- Support children's interests over time, reminding them of previous approaches and encouraging them to make connections between their experiences. CTC8

## Enabling environments

(What adults could provide)

Adults could provide additional support by:

- Providing stimulating resources which are accessible and open-ended so they can be used, moved and combined in a variety of ways. P&E1

- Making sure resources are relevant to children's interests. P&E2

- Helping children concentrate by limiting noise and making spaces visually calm and orderly. P&E4

- Noticing what arouses children's curiosity, looking for signs of deep involvement to identify learning that is intrinsically motivated. AL2

- Ensuring children have time and freedom to become deeply involved in activities. AL3

- Children can maintain focus on things that interest them over a period of time. Adults can help children to keep ideas in mind by talking over photographs of their previous activities. AL4

- In planning activities, adults could ask themselves: Is this an opportunity for children to find their own ways to represent and develop their own ideas? Avoid children just reproducing someone else's ideas. CTC1

- Recognisable and predictable routines help children to predict and make connections in their experiences. CTC4

- Routines can be flexible, while still basically orderly. CTC5

- Develop a learning community which focuses on how and not just what we are learning. CTC8

Encouraging a child to participate in an individual play experience is a way of helping them to regulate their behaviour and could be seen as a positive behaviour management strategy.

By having a number of the following individual play spaces, the children will have multiple opportunities to play alone, take some time out from friends, play and learn at their own level, learn to self-regulate their behaviour and enjoy moments of solitude.

## Light tables

Light tables are a great way to get children to explore, construct and discover new things. They add a fresh view to equipment, allowing children to create patterns, sort and categorise or simply be creative. They promote concentration, creativity and problem-solving skills.

*Taking time out to enjoy a moment of solitude.*

## A fairy land

Decorate your area with mosquito nets, gemstones, rocks, artificial or real flowers, mini logs, butterflies, pretty fabric table covers, artificial grass (or real would be nicer) fairies and more. These items came from the garden, art supply shops, pound shops, recycled materials and the charity shop.

## A bird table

A piece of hessian, an old organza curtain, some items from the garden and treasurers found in charity shops can look so inviting. In Spring and/or Autumn try going on a nature walk and collecting leaves, twigs, feathers and bits of straw to make a bird collage.

The owls and geese are the focus of these play experiences. They were all were found at a charity shop, along with the oil burner, jewelled pot and little plates. A plant or a mirror makes a lovely backdrop.

## A teddy bears' picnic

'One man's trash is another man's treasure' is the theme to these inspirational play spaces. Many of these objects were discovered in charity shops. These areas promote creativity, role-play, language development, sensory awareness and imagination.

# Under the sea

Shells and beads, fabric, gemstones, wooden boats and plastic sea creatures can be used to create a space that will fascinate and intrigue children. If you have an area outdoors for water play, provide sea-themed bath toys, shells and more for children to engage with in the water tray. Provide sea-themed books to take the learning further.

## Beads and marbles

Threading is a wonderful way to develop coordination in young children. Old dip platters provide an interesting divided tray to put the beads in.

The experience opposite was created using a non-slip bath mat, cut to the size of a tray. Stick the non-slip mat onto the tray with the suction cups facing up. Place a bowl of marbles on the table with some small tongs. The idea is for the children to move the marbles one by one from the bowl and place them onto the suction cups. This experience requires concentration, hand–eye coordination and fine motor control.

## Dinosaur world

Putting the plastic dinosaurs with pebbles, plants, grass and logs makes it more of an adventure.

## An arctic circle

For a multi-sensory experience, provide water, foam and polysrtyrene to create your own Arctic landscapes.

## A technology table

IT resources can be used throughout your setting to enhance the learning experiences you have on offer. Using donated calculators, computers, old mobile phones (without sim card), iPads, laptops, and more ideas such as these will support the children's learning.

*Pulling apart old electronic equipment is great for developing fine motor skills, language and social development, among many other things.*

## Sorting, categorising and more...

These experiences are designed to promote mathematical and scientific concepts such as sorting, categorising, ordering, colour mixing and comparing collections. They support the development of fine motor skills and have a calming effect on children.

Sorting and categorising using natural products is aesthetically pleasing as well as stimulating to the senses. Making patterns is a vital mathematical skill which can be supported by these activities.

# Chapter 8

# Construction

Children require access to construction activities to develop their fine motor coordination, problem-solving skills, creativity, social skills and language development. For many children, this is an area in which they feel most comfortable. They are able to easily express themselves while constructing, so it makes sense to have construction activities available to children at all times.

Giving children access to these experiences enables them to make their own choices. You can have rules about how many sets are allowed to be used at once, as this helps to develop their ability to negotiate and take turns.

## Early Learning Goals from the EYFS

**Playing with construction materials of various sizes and materials** enables children to work towards the following early learning goals. Key features of these that relate to construction are identified in italics:

### Personal, social and emotional development

Self-confidence and self-awareness:

Children are confident to try new activities, and say why they like some activities more than others. *They are confident to speak in a familiar group, will talk about their ideas, and will choose the resources they need for their chosen activities. They say when they do or don't need help.*

Managing feelings and behaviour:

Children talk about how they and others show feelings, talk about their own and others' behaviour, and its consequences, and know that some behaviour is unacceptable. *They work as part of a group or class, and understand and follow the rules.* They adjust their behaviour to different situations, and take changes of routine in their stride.

Making relationships:

*Children play co-operatively, taking turns with others. They take account of one another's ideas about how to organise their activity. They show sensitivity to others' needs and feelings, and form positive relationships with adults and other children.*

*Using a range of materials.*

### Communication and language

Speaking:

*Children express themselves effectively, showing awareness of listeners' needs.* They use past, present and future forms accurately when talking about events that have happened or are to happen in the future. *They develop their own narratives and explanations by connecting ideas or events.*

### Physical development

Moving and handling:

*Children show good control and co-ordination in large and small movements.* They move confidently in a range of ways, safely negotiating space. *They handle equipment and tools effectively, including pencils for writing.*

### Mathematics

Numbers:

*Children count reliably with numbers from 1 to 20*, place them in order and say which number is one more or one less than a given number. Using quantities and objects, they add and subtract two single-digit numbers and count on or back to find the answer. They solve problems, including doubling, halving and sharing.

Shape, space and measures:

*Children use everyday language to talk about size, weight, capacity, position, distance, time and money to compare quantities and objects and to solve problems. They recognise, create and describe patterns. They explore characteristics of everyday objects and shapes and use mathematical language to describe them.*

## Understanding the world

People and communities:

*Children talk about past and present events in their own lives and in the lives of family members*. They know that other children don't always enjoy the same things, and are sensitive to this. They know about similarities and differences between themselves and others, and among families, communities and traditions.

The world:

Children know about similarities and differences in relation to places, objects, materials and living things. *They talk about the features of their own immediate environment and how environments might vary from one another*. They make observations of animals and plants and explain why some things occur, and talk about changes.

## Expressive arts and design

Exploring and using media and materials:

Children sing songs, make music and dance, and experiment with ways of changing them. *They safely use and explore a variety of materials, tools and techniques, experimenting with colour, design, texture, form and function*.

Being imaginative:

*Children use what they have learnt about media and materials in original ways, thinking about uses and purposes. They represent their own ideas, thoughts and feelings through design and technology*, art, music, dance, role-play and stories.

*Helping a friend makes us feel happy, healthy, safe and connected to others.*

## Characteristics of Effective Learning

When children are learning through play with construction resources, adults will be able to observe some of the Characteristics of Effective Learning from the EYFS. In this section, the photos are accompanied by some of these 'CEL' statements:

*(Note: In the following text, P&E = Playing and Exploring; AL = Active Learning; CTC= Creating and Thinking Critically)*

## The unique child

(observing how a child is learning)

Children may:

- Use senses to explore the world around them. P&E2

- Engage in open-ended activity. P&E3

- Represent their experiences in play. P&E6

- Act out experiences with other people. P&E8

- Initiate activities. P&E9

- Show a 'can do' attitude. P&E11

- Maintain focus on their activity for a period of time. AL1

- Show high levels of energy, fascination. AL2

- Pay attention to details. AL4

- Show a belief that more effort or a different approach will pay off. AL6

- Be proud of how they accomplished something – not just the end result. AL9

- Thinking of ideas. CTC1

- Find ways to solve problems. CTC2

- Make predictions CTC5

- Test their ideas. CTC6

## Positive relationships

(What adults could do)

Adults may:

- Play with children. Encourage them to explore, and showing their own interest in discovering new things. P&E1

- Help children as needed to do what they are trying to do, without taking over or directing. P&E2

- Talk about how you and the children get better at things through effort and practice, and what we all can learn when things go wrong. P&E7

- Stimulate children's interest through shared attention, and calming over-stimulated children. AL2

- Be specific when praising, especially noting effort such as how the child concentrates, tries different approaches, persists, solves problems, and has new ideas. AL4

- Encourage children to learn together, and from each other. AL5

- Use the language of thinking and learning: think, know, remember, forget, idea, makes sense, plan, learn, find out, confused, figure out, trying to do. CTC1

- Encourage open-ended thinking by not settling on the first ideas: *What else is possible?* CTC3

- Always respect children's efforts and ideas, so they feel safe to take a risk with a new idea. CTC4

- Model the creative process, by showing their own thinking about some of the many possible ways forward. CTC8

- Follow children's lead in conversation, and think about things together. Sustained shared thinking helps children to explore ideas and make links. CTC9

- Encourage children to describe problems they encounter, and to suggest ways to solve the problem. CTC10

*Developing the ability to share.*

## Enabling environments

(What adults could provide)

Adults could provide additional support by:

- Offering stimulating resources which are accessible and open-ended so they can be used, moved and combined in a variety of ways. P&E1

- Arranging flexible indoor and outdoor space and resources where children can explore, build, move and role-play. P&E3

- Ensuring children have uninterrupted time to play and explore. P&E6

- Children will become more deeply involved when adults provide something that is new and unusual for them to explore, especially when it is linked to their interests. AL1

- Children can maintain focus on things that interest them over a period of time. Adults can help children to keep ideas in mind by talking over photographs of their previous activities. AL4

- In planning activities, adults could ask themselves: *Is this an opportunity for children to find their own ways to represent and develop their own ideas?* CTC1

- Building in opportunities for children to play with materials before using them in planned tasks. CTC2

- Play is a key opportunity for children to think creatively and flexibly, solve problems and link ideas. Adults can promote the enabling conditions for rich play: space, time, flexible resources, choice, control, warm and supportive relationships. CTC3

## Duplo and Lego

Duplo and Lego are excellent construction sets for young children, encouraging them to develop fine motor skills, hand–eye coordination and problem-solving skills. Sharing is a tricky skill to learn at any age, and these construction sets really help children develop the ability to negotiate and share.

Both sets can be played with either at a table or on the floor and are a popular choice for all children. Duplo is a larger block and may be more suitable for younger children. Lego is smaller and more difficult to manipulate, therefore is more suitable for children over the age of four. Depending on the skill of the children, adult supervision and interests of the group, both construction sets will be extremely useful and popular.

## Wooden blocks

Occasionally it is a good idea to set up the block area in advance to encourage children and give them a starting point for their play. This is also helpful when supporting particular learning that may be occurring for the children at that time, such as following a visit to the zoo.

Adding other props makes the experience more interesting and extends the play. Photographs pinned to the wall show children what props are available to them, and adding live plants and even water helps children explore their senses while playing here.

Including clipboards with paper and pencils or covering a wall in paper allows children to draw or design what they are making. This is ideal for the reluctant drawer as they don't have to go to a drawing table.

## Train sets

Train sets allow children to use thinking strategies and fine motor coordination, while also supporting social skills and problem-solving skills.

## Large blocks

Large blocks can be used indoors and outdoors and are wonderful for making play houses, planes, buses and other great construction to get in to. Large block play encourages team work.

## Woodwork

Children can create wonderful masterpieces with materials from your local hardware store or recycling point. Using a hammer and nails works fine and gross motor skills at the same time as well as developing hand–eye coordination.

## Box construction

This is a construction activity that will keep children busy creating and exploring all year round. Children can make almost anything out of recycled cardboard boxes!

Creating a box construction city is a lot of fun, and group projects such as these are great at getting the group to think and talk together to develop shared outcomes. Having 'town planning' meetings together allow children to share ideas and learn new ways of thinking and being.

Inspiring Play Spaces

# Chapter 9

# Painting

Children are naturally creative beings. They are uninhibited and egocentric and when told their work is beautiful they will believe you and go back to do more. Even the child who is reluctant to try because they say they can't paint will, with a little encouragement and praise, have a go – and the smile you see on their face when they realise how talented they are as an artist is a priceless moment in teaching.

## Early Learning Goals from the EYFS

**Painting and other mark–making experiences** enable children to work towards the following early learning goals. Key features of these that relate to painting are identified in *italics*:

### Personal, social and emotional development

Self-confidence and self-awareness:

*Children are confident to try new activities, and say why they like some activities more than others*. They are confident to speak in a familiar group, will talk about their ideas, and will choose the resources they need for their chosen activities. They say when they do or don't need help.

Managing feelings and behaviour:

*Children talk about how they and others show feelings, talk about their own and others' behaviour* and its consequences, and know that some behaviour is unacceptable. They work as part of a group or class, and understand and follow the rules. They adjust their behaviour to different situations, and take changes of routine in their stride.

## Physical development

Moving and handling:

*Children show good control and co-ordination in large and small movements*. They move confidently in a range of ways, safely negotiating space. *They handle equipment and tools effectively, including pencils for writing.*

## Understanding the world

People and communities:

*Children talk about past and present events in their own lives and in the lives of family members*. They know that other children don't always enjoy the same things, and are sensitive to this. They know about similarities and differences between themselves and others, and among families, communities and traditions.

The world:

*Children know about similarities and differences in relation to places, objects, materials and living things. They talk about the features of their own immediate environment and how environments might vary from one another*. They make observations of animals and plants and explain why some things occur, and talk about changes.

## Technology

Children recognise that a range of technology is used in places such as homes and schools. *They select and use technology for particular purposes.*

## Expressive arts and design

Exploring and using media and materials:

Children sing songs, make music and dance, and experiment with ways of changing them. *They safely use and explore a variety of materials, tools and techniques, experimenting with colour, design, texture, form and function.*

Being imaginative:

*Children use what they have learnt about media and materials in original ways, thinking about uses and purposes. They represent their own ideas*, thoughts and feelings through design and technology, *art*, music, dance, role-play and stories.

*Connecting with others on a group project.*

# Characteristics of Effective Learning

When children are learning through painting and other mark making, adults will be able to observe some of the Characteristics of Effective Learning from the EYFS). In this section, the photos are accompanied by some of these 'CEL' statements:

*(Note: In the following text, P&E = Playing and Exploring; AL = Active Learning; CTC= Creating and Thinking Critically)*

## The unique child

(observing how a child is learning)

Children may:

- Show curiosity about objects, events and people. P&E1

- Use senses to explore the world around them. P&E2

- Represent their experiences in play. P&E6

- Show a 'can do' attitude. P&E11

- Take a risk, engage in new experiences, and learn by trial and error. P&E12

- Maintain focus on their activity for a period of time. AL1

- Pay attention to details. AL4

- Persist with activity when challenges occur. AL5

- Be proud of how they accomplished something – not just the end result. AL9

- Think of ideas. CTC1

- Test their ideas. CTC5

- Plan, make decisions about how to approach a task, solve a problem and reach a goal. CTC7

## Positive relationships

(What adults could do)

Adults may:

- Help children as needed to do what they are trying to do, without taking over or directing. P&E2

- Encourage children to try new activities and to judge risks for themselves. Be sure to support children's confidence with words and body language. P&E5

- Support children to choose their activities – what they want to do and how they will do it. AL1

- Help children to become aware of their own goals, make plans, and review their own progress and successes. Describe what they see children trying to do, and encouraging children to talk about their own processes and successes. AL3

- Be specific when praising, especially noting effort such as how the child concentrates, tries different approaches, persists, solves problems, and has new ideas. AL4

- Use the language of thinking and learning: *think, know, remember, forget, idea, makes sense, plan, learn, find out, confused, figure out, trying to do.* CTC1

- Always respect children's efforts and ideas, so they feel safe to take a risk with a new idea. CTC4

- Give children time to talk and think. CTC6

- Encourage children to describe problems they encounter, and to suggest ways to solve the problem. CTC11

- Show and talk about strategies – how to do things – including problem-solving, thinking and learning. CTC12

## Enabling environments

(What adults could provide)

Adults could provide additional support by:

- Providing stimulating resources which are accessible and open-ended so they can be used, moved and combined in a variety of ways. P&E1

- Making sure resources are relevant to children's interests. P&E2

- Arranging flexible indoor and outdoor space and resources where children can explore, build, move and role play. P&E3

- Ensuring children have uninterrupted time to play and explore. P&E6

- Children will become more deeply involved when adults provide something that is new and unusual for them to explore, especially when it is linked to their interests. AL1

- Ensuring children have time and freedom to become deeply involved in activities. AL3

- In planning activities, adults could ask themselves: *Is this an opportunity for children to find their own ways to represent and develop their own ideas?* Avoid children just reproducing someone else's ideas. CTC1

- Play is a key opportunity for children to think creatively and flexibly, solve problems and link ideas. Adults can promote the enabling conditions for rich play: space, time, flexible resources, choice, control, warm and supportive relationships. CTC3

- Recognisable and predictable routines help children to predict and make connections in their experiences. CTC4

- Plan linked experiences that follow the ideas children are really thinking about. CTC6

- Use mind-maps to represent thinking together. CTC7

- Develop a learning community which focuses on how and not just what we are learning. CTC8

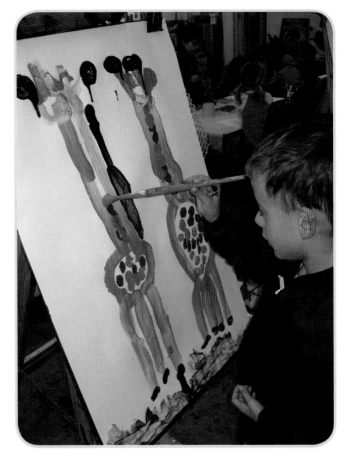

*Visiting the zoo and other exciting venues encourages children to paint new things.*

*Children were inspired to paint animals when toys were placed near the easel.*

# Easel painting

It is not just a matter of putting paints next to an easel and thinking that's it for easel painting. This area of your room needs to be continually changing to remain inviting and stimulating. Here are some ideas for making the easel area become a hive of activity and creativity.

*Finger painting works well using a see-through easel.*

*Adding glue sticks to the painting at the easel activity provides a new medium, allowing children to experience new textures.*

*I.T. can be used to enhance the experience and provide visual stimulation.*

## Murals and canvases

Providing children with a canvas to paint on shows them how much you value them as artists. Many of the children's paintings were sold at our art show to raise money for the kindergarten.

*Group finger painting outdoors.*

*This mural created the backdrop to our box construction city.*

# Printing

**Bubble printing** is very messy but a lot of fun. Put non-toxic washing-up liquid into three paint pots, fill a third of the pot with water and add food colouring. Provide a fresh straw for each child and have plenty of paper towel on hand. Don't forget the aprons!

Before allowing children to blow in the water with the straw, make sure they practise blowing through them onto their hands. It is a natural instinct to suck through a straw.

Once the child has blown a tall pile of bubbles, they place a piece of paper on top of the pot and print the bubbles onto the paper. Repeat with the other colours. It has a lovely effect and helps children to follow instruction, concentrate and try something new.

For **golf ball printing**, place a golf ball in a bowl of paint then transfer to a baking tray, with paper lining the bottom. The child rolls the ball around in the baking tray, creating tracks or marks on their paper. Using more than one colour creates a great effect.

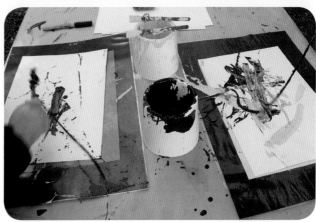

Try **wool printing** by tying a 30cm length of wool onto an ice lolly stick and lowering it into a pot of paint. Encourage the children to 'dance' or 'bounce' the wool on the paper will ensure the colours don't get mixed together creating a brown painting. This activity is good for practising coordination and following instructions.

## Overhead projectors

By projecting the children's drawings you can enlarge them to create magnificent murals. Many schools are throwing out old overhead projectors and upgrading to data projectors, so contact schools in your area to see if they would donate one to your setting.

In this activity, the children painted on clear projector sheets and could see their artwork blown up in front of them on the wall.

## Painted boxes

Extend the box construction activity on page 50 by offering the children the opportunity to paint the masterpieces. This is a great way of helping them see their art as an ongoing project and getting them to think of other ways to extend their ideas.

## Watercolours

Using child-friendly dye, food colouring or pallet paints, painting with water creates very beautiful effects.

## Visiting artists

Inviting people to visit your setting and do art with the children not only opens their mind to new ideas but allows them to watch and learn new ways of being. By watching a visiting artist paint (or construct, draw, mould, hammer ....) the children will learn new ways to explore paint and may even try something new. From time to time, sit and paint with the children yourself; not only is it relaxing but it affirms the belief that you respect and value what the children do.

# Chapter 10

# Scissors, glue and collage

Cutting and sticking has been a favourite experience in early childhood settings for many years. It is the free and open-ended discovery of craft items, the textures, shapes, colours and treasures that can be found on the craft table that are so inviting.

One of the focuses of the EYFS is for children to have access to equipment and resources, highlighting the importance of having these craft items in your setting. You may wish to provide a shelf or trolley with separate containers or baskets with a variety of bits and bobs for children to choose from. There are many clever ways to bring the craft items out of the cupboard to display in an inviting way for children to access themselves.

*Being able to choose the materials for pasting provides a sense of ownership.*

## Early Learning Goals from the EYFS

**Exploring cutting, glue and collage** enables children to work towards the following early learning goals. Particular features of these are identified in ***italics***:

### Personal, social and emotional development

Self-confidence and self-awareness:

***Children are confident to try new activities, and say why they like some activities more than others.*** They are confident to speak in a familiar group, will talk about their ideas, and will choose the resources they need for their chosen activities. ***They say when they do or don't need help.***

Managing feelings and behaviour:

Children talk about how they and others show feelings, talk about their own and others' behaviour, and its consequences, and know that some behaviour is unacceptable. ***They work as part of a group or class, and understand and follow the rules. They adjust their behaviour to different situations, and take changes of routine in their stride.***

Making relationships:

***Children play co-operatively, taking turns with others. They take account of one another's ideas about how to organise their activity.*** They show sensitivity to others' needs and feelings, and form positive relationships with adults and other children.

## Communication and language

Speaking:

*Children express themselves effectively*, showing awareness of listeners' needs. They use past, present and future forms accurately when talking about events that have happened or are to happen in the future. *They develop their own narratives and explanations by connecting ideas or events.*

## Physical development

Moving and handling:

*Children show good control and co-ordination in large and small movements.* They move confidently in a range of ways, safely negotiating space. *They handle equipment and tools effectively, including pencils for writing.*

## Mathematics

Shape, space and measures:

*Children use everyday language to talk about size*, weight, capacity, position, distance, time and money to compare quantities and objects and to solve problems. They recognise, create and describe patterns. *They explore characteristics of everyday objects and shapes and use mathematical language to describe them.*

## Understanding the world

People and communities:

Children talk about past and present events in their own lives and in the lives of family members. *They know that other children don't always enjoy the same things, and are sensitive to this.* They know about similarities and differences between themselves and others, and among families, communities and traditions.

## Expressive arts and design

Exploring and using media and materials:

Children sing songs, make music and dance, and experiment with ways of changing them. *They safely use and explore a variety of materials, tools and techniques, experimenting with colour, design, texture, form and function.*

Being imaginative:

Children use what they have learnt about media and materials in original ways, thinking about uses and purposes. *They represent their own ideas, thoughts and feelings through* design and technology, *art*, music, dance, role-play and stories.

# Characteristics of Effective Learning

When children are learning through play with cutting, glue and collage, adults will be able to observe some of the Characteristics of Effective Learning from the EYFS. In this section, the photos are accompanied by some of these 'CEL' statements:

*(Note: In the following text, P&E = Playing and Exploring; AL = Active Learning; CTC= Creating and Thinking Critically)*

## The unique child

(observing how a child is learning)

Children may:

- Show curiosity about objects, events and people. P&E1

- Use senses to explore the world around them. P&E2

- Engage in open-ended activity. P&E3

- Represent their experiences in play. P&E6

- Show a 'can do' attitude. P&E11

- Pay attention to details. AL4

- Persist with activity when challenges occur. AL5

- Be proud of how they accomplished something – not just the end result. AL9

- Think of ideas. CTC1

- Find ways to solve problems. CTC2

- Test their ideas. CTC6

- Plan, making decisions about how to approach a task, solve a problem and reach a goal. CT8

- Check how well their activities are going. CTC9

- Change strategy as needed. CTC10

- Review how well the approach worked. CTC11

## Positive relationships

(What adults could do)

Adults may:

- Help children as needed to do what they are trying to do, without taking over or directing. P&E2

- Join in play sensitively, fitting in with children's ideas. P&E3

- Encourage children to try new activities and to judge risks for themselves. Be sure to support children's confidence with words and body language. P&E5

- Support children to choose their activities – what they want to do and how they will do it. AL1

- Help children to become aware of their own goals, make plans, and review their own progress and successes.

- Be specific when praising, especially noting effort such as how the child concentrates, tries different approaches, persists, solves problems, and has new ideas. AL4

- Use the language of thinking and learning: think, know, remember, forget, idea, makes sense, plan, learn, find out, confused, figure out, trying to do. CTC1

- Encourage open-ended thinking by not settling on the first ideas: What else is possible? CTC3

- Always respect children's efforts and ideas, so they feel safe to take a risk with a new idea. CTC4

- Model the creative process, by showing their own thinking about some of the many possible ways forward. CTC9

- Follow children's lead in conversation, and thinking about things together. Sustained shared thinking helps children to explore ideas and make links.. CTC10

- Give feedback and help children to review their own progress and learning. Talking with children about what they are doing, how they plan to do it, what worked well and what they would change next time. CTC11

*Access to materials encourages creativity.*

## Enabling environments

(What adults could provide)

Adults could provide additional support by:

- Offering stimulating resources which are accessible and open-ended so they can be used, moved and combined in a variety of ways. P&E1

- Making sure resources are relevant to children's interests. P&E2

- Arranging flexible indoor and outdoor space and resources where children can explore, build, move and role play. P&E3

- Ensuring children have uninterrupted time to play and explore. P&E6

- Noticing what arouses children's curiosity, looking for signs of deep involvement to identify learning that is intrinsically motivated. AL2

- Ensuring children have time and freedom to become deeply involved in activities. AL3

- Keeping significant activities out instead of routinely tidying them away. AL5

- In planning activities, adults could ask themselves: *Is this an opportunity for children to find their own ways to represent and develop their own ideas?* Avoid children just reproducing someone else's ideas. CTC1

- Use mind-maps to represent thinking together. CTC7

- Develop a learning community which focuses on how and not just what we are learning. CTC8

## Extended box construction

Children rarely tire of this experience due to its open-ended nature. There are no limits to what can be created here – whether it's construction or deconstruction! Not only are children free to create, but they have access to sticky tape, scissors, glue and a variety of inviting craft bits and pieces.

If you have limited space or are unable to provide access to craft supplies, this is a wonderful way to offer a wide variety of items in a very small space.

## Collage

The children in this group had developed an interest in frogs. Using some rocks, paint, goggle eyes and paper, they were able to draw and cut out their own frogs' legs.

Only one child worked with the practitioner at a time for this experience, but the table was so beautiful that other children enjoyed sitting and playing with the decorative items while they waited.

## Working with natural objects

There are so many ways of exploring nature through art. The children were engrossed in designing and creating animals using objects such as sticks, leaves and pine cones. As the hot glue gun was required, an practitioner's help was needed to stick it all together, but the children decided where things were to go and what items would be used.

# Chapter 11

# Reading areas

## Early Learning Goals from the EYFS

Reading areas are a vital component of any early years setting, and practitioners should take as much care about their appeal as they do with any other area of learning. Spending time in reading and book areas enables children to work towards the following early learning goals. Key features of these that relate to reading are identified in *italics*:

### Personal, social and emotional development

Self-confidence and self-awareness:

Children are confident to try new activities, and say why they like some activities more than others. *They are confident to speak in a familiar group, will talk about their ideas, and will choose the resources they need for their chosen activities.* They say when they do or don't need help.

Managing feelings and behaviour:

Children talk about how they and others show feelings, talk about their own and others' behaviour, and its consequences, and know that some behaviour is unacceptable. *They work as part of a group or class, and understand and follow the rules. They adjust their behaviour to different situations, and take changes of routine in their stride.*

Making relationships:

*Children play co-operatively, taking turns with others.* They take account of one another's ideas about how to organise their activity. They show sensitivity to others' needs and feelings, and *form positive relationships with adults and other children.*

*Bringing in a favourite book.*

### Communication and language

Listening and attention:

*Children listen attentively in a range of situations. They listen to stories, accurately anticipating key events and respond to what they hear with relevant comments, questions or actions. They give their attention to what others say and respond appropriately, while engaged in another activity.*

Understanding:

Children follow instructions involving several ideas or actions. *They answer 'how' and 'why' questions about their experiences and in response to stories or events.*

Speaking:

Children express themselves effectively, showing awareness of listeners' needs. *They use past, present and future forms accurately when talking about events that have happened or are to happen in the future. They develop their own narratives and explanations by connecting ideas or events.*

## Physical development

**Moving and handling:**

Children show good control and co-ordination in large and small movements. They move confidently in a range of ways, safely negotiating space. They handle equipment and tools effectively, including pencils for writing.

## Literacy

**Reading:**

Children read and understand simple sentences. They use phonic knowledge to decode regular words and read them aloud accurately. They also read some common irregular words. They demonstrate understanding when talking with others about what they have read.

## Understanding the world

**People and communities:**

Children talk about past and present events in their own lives and in the lives of family members. They know that other children don't always enjoy the same things, and are sensitive to this. They know about similarities and differences between themselves and others, and among families, communities and traditions.

## Technology

Children recognise that a range of technology is used in places such as homes and schools. They select and use technology for particular purposes.

## Expressive arts and design

**Being imaginative:**

Children use what they have learnt about media and materials in original ways, thinking about uses and purposes. They represent their own ideas, thoughts and feelings through design and technology, art, music, dance, role-play and stories.

*Reading books alone allows us to enjoy important moments of solitude.*

## Characteristics of effective learning

When children are learning through experiences with books, adults will be able to observe some of the Characteristics of Effective Learning from the EYFS. In this section, the photos are accompanied by some of these 'CEL' statements:

*(Note: In the following text, P&E = Playing and Exploring; AL = Active Learning; CTC= Creating and Thinking Critically)*

## The unique child

(observing how a child is learning)

**Children may:**

- Show curiosity about objects, events and people. P&E1

- Use senses to explore the world around them. P&E2

- Show particular interests. P&E4

- Seek challenge. P&E10

- Take a risk, engage in new experiences, and learning by trial and error. P&E12

- Maintain focus on their activity for a period of time. AL1

- Show high levels of energy, fascination. AL2

- Be not easily distracted. AL3

- Pay attention to details. AL4

- Be proud of how they accomplished something – not just the end result. AL9

- Enjoy meeting challenges for their own sake rather than external rewards or praise. AL10

- Make links and notice patterns in their experience. CTC3

- Plan, make decisions about how to approach a task, solve a problem and reach a goal. CTC8

## Positive relationships

(What adults could do)

Adults may:

- Play with children. Encouraging them to explore, and showing their own interest in discovering new things. P&E1

- Help children as needed to do what they are trying to do, without taking over or directing. P&E2

- Join in play sensitively, fitting in with children's ideas. P&E3

- Model pretending an object is something else, and help develop roles and stories. P&E4

- Encourage children to try new activities and to judge risks for themselves. Be sure to support children's confidence with words and body language. P&E5

- Talk about how you and the children get better at things through effort and practice, and what we all can learn when things go wrong. P&E7

- Encourage children to learn together, and from each other. AL5

- Use the language of thinking and learning: *think, know, remember, forget, idea, makes sense, plan, learn, find out, confused, figure out, trying to do.* CTC1

- Always respect children's efforts and ideas, so they feel safe to take a risk with a new idea. CTC4

- Talking aloud helps children to think and control what they do. Adults should model self-talk, describing their actions in play.

- Value questions, talk, and many possible responses, without rushing toward answers too quickly. CTC7

- Sustained shared thinking helps children to explore ideas and make links. Follow children's lead in conversation, and think about things together. CTC10

- Give feedback and help children to review their own progress and learning. Talk with children about what they are doing, how they plan to do it, what worked well and what they would change next time. CTC12

## Enabling environments

(What adults could provide)

Adults could provide additional support by:

- Offering stimulating resources which are accessible and open-ended so they can be used, moved and combined in a variety of ways. P&E1

- Making sure resources are relevant to children's interests. P&E2

- Arranging flexible indoor and outdoor space and resources where children can explore, build, move and role play. P&E3

- Helping children concentrate by limiting noise and making spaces visually calm and orderly. P&E4

- Ensuring children have uninterrupted time to play and explore. P&E6

- Children will become more deeply involved when adults provide something that is new and unusual for them to explore, especially when it is linked to their interests. AL1

- Noticing what arouses children's curiosity, looking for signs of deep involvement to identify learning that is intrinsically motivated. AL2

- Ensuring children have time and freedom to become deeply involved in activities. AL3

- Recognisable and predictable routines help children to predict and make connections in their experiences. CTC4

- Routines can be flexible, while still basically orderly. CTC5

- Plan linked experiences that follow the ideas children are really thinking about. CTC6

- Use mind-maps to represent thinking together. CTC7

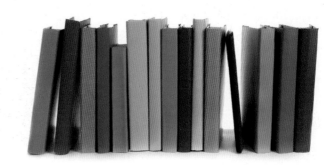

The most important thing about reading areas is to have a variety of well-maintained books available. Books with tatty covers in bad condition, with ripped or shabby edges, are not appealing to look at or inviting to read.

Children need to be taught how to care for books. Teach them that books do not belong on the ground, but on a shelf or in a basket where they will be safe. Teach children how to turn pages carefully so that they do not get ripped.

Books are wonderful for supporting the learning going on in your setting at all times. Reading areas can be made available to children both indoors and outdoors, and providing books to support each child's interests is achievable and very important. If your setting does not have a large or varied book collection, then join your local library and borrow books to meet the needs and interests of the children in your care.

*Reading to children provides opportunities for intentional teaching.*

Families may be able to donate books – either used or new. Another way to build up a variety of books is to invite children to bring their favourite book from home. Maybe you could provide a 'library bag' that goes home with one child each day. Children learn that books are so special they get a bag to travel in.

Celebrating book week is another way of discovering children's interests. They can dress up as their favourite book character and bring in the book that inspired them. You could arrange with the local school to visit the library on a fortnightly or monthly basis. Walk the children to the library with their library bags and borrow books, then return them a fortnight later. Not only does this support children's transition to school and develop links with your local community, it also provides you with many lovely books to read.

Inviting reading areas should include a comfortable place to sit. They should have lots of natural light, and a variety of books either on a shelf or in a basket. It is a good idea to have somewhere for adults to sit too, as taking a few minutes to read to children during the day not only supports their development in so many areas but also teaches children that adults value reading.

Transforming your book corner into a library and teaching children about the possibilities and opportunities of becoming a member of the local library will mean you are supporting their learning potential out of the setting too.

# Chapter 12

# Cooking

Including cooking activities in your setting promotes language development and mathematical concepts such as an understanding of volume, capacity, measurement and quantity, turn-taking and other social skills, as well as a sense of belonging.

Cooking is a wonderful way of supporting cultures of the families at your setting. Inviting families to come and cook with the children and share recipes from their culture broadens our understanding of the community and supports everyone in feeling a sense of belonging, respect and connectedness.

Always put the children's safety first – never leave hot pans or other dangerous cooking equipment unattended.

## Early Learning Goals from the EYFS

Cooking and other food preparation experiences enable children to work towards the following early learning goals. Key features of these that relate to cooking are identified in *italics*:

### Personal, social and emotional development

Self-confidence and self-awareness:

*Children are confident to try new activities, and say why they like some activities more than others.* They are confident to speak in a familiar group, will talk about their ideas, and *will choose the resources they need for their chosen activities. They say when they do or don't* need help.

Managing feelings and behaviour:

Children talk about how they and others show feelings, talk about their own and others' behaviour, and its consequences, and know that some behaviour is unacceptable. *They work as part of a group or class, and understand and follow the rules. They adjust their behaviour to different situations, and take changes of routine in their stride.*

Making relationships:

Children play co-operatively, taking turns with others. *They take account of one another's ideas about how to organise their activity.* They show sensitivity to others' needs and feelings, and form positive relationships with adults and other children.

*Cooking using food colouring.*

## Communication and language

Listening and attention:

*Children listen attentively in a range of situations*. They listen to stories, accurately anticipating key events and respond to what they hear with relevant comments, questions or actions. They give their attention to what others say and respond appropriately, while engaged in another activity.

Understanding:

*Children follow instructions involving several ideas or actions*. They answer 'how' and 'why' questions about their experiences and in response to stories or events.

Speaking:

Children express themselves effectively, showing awareness of listeners' needs. They use past, present and future forms accurately when talking about events that have happened or are to happen in the future. *They develop their own narratives and explanations by connecting ideas or events.*

## Physical development

Moving and handling:

*Children show good control and co-ordination in large and small movements.* They move confidently in a range of ways, safely negotiating space. *They handle equipment and tools effectively, including pencils for writing.*

Health and self-care:

*Children know the importance for good health of physical exercise, and a healthy diet, and talk about ways to keep healthy and safe.* They manage their own basic hygiene and personal needs successfully, including dressing and going to the toilet independently.

*Working together as a group.*

*Learning to do new things makes us feel competent and capable.*

## Mathematics

Numbers:

*Children count reliably with numbers from 1 to 20*, place them in order and say which number is one more or one less than a given number. Using quantities and objects, they add and subtract two single-digit numbers and count on or back to find the answer. They solve problems, including doubling, halving and sharing.

## Undestanding the world

People and communities:

*Children talk about past and present events in their own lives and in the lives of family members. They know that other children don't always enjoy the same things, and are sensitive to this.* They know about similarities and differences between themselves and others, and among families, communities and traditions.

## Technology

*Children recognise that a range of technology is used in places such as homes and schools. They select and use technology for particular purposes.*

## Expressive arts and design

Exploring and using media and materials:

Children sing *songs, make music and dance, and experiment with ways of changing them. They safely use and explore a variety of materials, tools and techniques,* experimenting with colour, design, texture, form and function.

# Characteristics of Effective Learning

When children are learning through cooking and other food preparation experiences, adults will be able to observe some of the Characteristics of Effective Learning from the Early Years Foundation Stage (England). In this section, the photos are accompanied by some of these 'CEL' statements:

*(Note: In the following text, P&E = Playing and Exploring; AL = Active Learning; CTC= Creating and Thinking Critically)*

## The unique child

(observing how a child is learning)

Children may:

- Show curiosity about objects, events and people. P&E1

- Use senses to explore the world around them. P&E2

- Seek challenge. P&E10

- Show a 'can do' attitude. P&E11

- Maintain focus on their activity for a period of time. AL1

- Show high levels of energy, fascination. AL2

- Pay attention to details. AL4

- Show satisfaction in meeting their own goals. AL8

- Be proud of how they accomplished something – not just the end result.  AL9

- Find ways to solve problems. CTC2

- Make predictions. CTC5

- Plan, make decisions about how to approach a task, solve a problem and reach a goal. CTC8

- Check how well their activities are going. CTC9

- Review how well the approach worked. CTC11

## Positive relationships

(What adults could do)

Adults may:

- Help children as needed to do what they are trying to do, without taking over or directing. P&E2

- Encourage children to try new activities and to judge risks for themselves. Be sure to support children's confidence with words and body language. P&E5

- Talk about how you and the children get better at things through effort and practice, and what we all can learn when things go wrong. P&E7

- Be specific when praising, especially noting effort such as how the child concentrates, tries different approaches, persists, solves problems, and has new ideas. AL4

- Encourage children to learn together, and from each other. AL5

- Use the language of thinking and learning: think, know, remember, forget, idea, makes sense, plan, learn, find out, confused, figure out, trying to do. CTC1

- Encourage open-ended thinking by not settling on the first ideas: *What else is possible?* CTC3

- Always respect children's efforts and ideas, so they feel safe to take a risk with a new idea. CTC4

- Value questions, talk, and many possible responses, without rushing toward answers too quickly. CTC7

- Model the creative process, by showing their own thinking about some of the many possible ways forward. CTC9

- Encourage children to describe problems they encounter, and to suggest ways to solve the problem. CTC11

- Show and talk about strategies – how to do things – including problem-solving, thinking and learning. CTC12

## Enabling environments
(What adults could provide)

Adults could provide additional support by:

- Offering stimulating resources which are accessible and open-ended so they can be used, moved and combined in a variety of ways. P&E1

- Planning first-hand experiences and challenges appropriate to the development of the children. P&E5

- Children will become more deeply involved when adults provide something that is new and unusual for them to explore, especially when it is linked to their interests. AL1

- Ensuring children have time and freedom to become deeply involved in activities. AL3

- In planning activities, adults could ask themselves: Is this an opportunity for children to find their own ways to represent and develop their own ideas? Avoid children just reproducing someone else's ideas. CTC1

- Recognisable and predictable routines help children to predict and make connections in their experiences. CTC4

- Plan linked experiences that follow the ideas children are really thinking about. CTC5

- Develop a learning community which focuses on how and not just what we are learning. CTC8

It is important to prepare carefully for a cooking experience as you need to be aware of the allergies and dietary requirements of the children in your care. There are many products available that allow you to cook, even with children with food allergies. You can buy dairy-free margarine, gluten-free flour, egg replacer and many more options to cater for all the specific needs of individual children. Always remember to wash hands before you start cooking to avoid cross contamination.

Providing families with a copy of the recipe that you will be using that day is a good idea. This means that children can cook with their parents at home too. Inviting families to cook traditional meals reflecting their culture allows children to take risks and try something new.

The chefs hats used here allow the children to role-play while participating in the cooking experience.

*Participating in cooking experiences supports our ability to make choices and influence the program.*

# Chapter 13

# Sand and digging areas

This chapter looks at the sandpit, sand kitchens and digging patches. The sandpit is self-explanatory, and is probably one of the first things built in every early childhood setting.

The sand kitchen refers to the area where children can make and cook sand cakes, casseroles, drinks and other delicious sandy treats! The digging patch is any area of dirt where children can dig, make mud and splash in!

These are just some of the ways in which sandpit and digging patch experiences support children's learning and development.

*The sand kitchen encourages interactions with others.*

## Early Learning Goals from the EYFS

Playing with sand, soil and compost enables children to work towards the following early learning goals. Key features of these that relate to sand play are identified in *italics*:

### Personal, social and emotional development

Self-confidence and self-awareness:

*Children are confident to try new activities, and say why they like some activities more than others*. They are confident to speak in a familiar group, will talk about their ideas, and will choose the resources they need for their chosen activities. They say when they do or don't need help.

### Managing feelings and behaviour

Children talk about how they and others show feelings, talk about their own and others' behaviour and its consequences, and know that some behaviour is unacceptable. *They work as part of a group or class, and understand and follow the rules*. They adjust their behaviour to different situations, and take changes of routine in their stride.

Making relationships:

*Children play co-operatively, taking turns with others. They take account of one another's ideas about how to organise their activity*. They show sensitivity to others' needs and feelings, and form positive relationships with adults and other children.

### Communication and language

Understanding:

Children follow instructions involving several ideas or actions. *They answer 'how' and 'why' questions about their experiences and in response to stories or events*.

Speaking:

Children express themselves effectively, showing awareness of listeners' needs. They use past, present and future forms accurately when talking about events that have happened or are to happen in the future. *They develop their own narratives and explanations by connecting ideas or events*.

### Physical development

Moving and handling:

*Children show good control and co-ordination in large and small movements. They move confidently in a range of ways, safely negotiating space. They handle equipment and tools effectively*, including pencils for writing.

### Mathematics

Shape, space and measures:

*Children use everyday language to talk about size, weight, capacity, position*, distance, time and money to compare quantities and objects and to solve problems. They recognise, create and describe patterns. They explore characteristics of everyday objects and shapes and use mathematical language to describe them.

### Understanding the world

The world:

Children know about similarities and differences in relation to places, objects, materials and living things. *They talk about the features of their own immediate environment and how environments might vary from one another*. They make observations of animals and plants and explain why some things occur, and talk about changes.

### Expressive arts and design

Exploring and using media and materials:

Children sing songs, make music and dance, and experiment with ways of changing them. *They safely use and explore a variety of materials, tools and techniques*, experimenting with colour, design, texture, form and function.

Being imaginative:

Children use what they have learnt about media and materials in original ways, thinking about uses and purposes. *They represent their own ideas, thoughts and feelings through* design and technology, art, music, dance, role-play and *stories*.

## Characteristics of Effective Learning

When children are learning through play with sand, soil and compost, adults will be able to observe some of the Characteristics of Effective Learning from the EYFS. In this section, the photos are accompanied by some of these 'CEL' statements:

*(Note: In the following text, P&E = Playing and Exploring; AL = Active Learning; CTC= Creating and Thinking Critically)*

### The unique child

(observing how a child is learning)

Children may:

- Use senses to explore the world around them. P&E2

- Engage in open-ended activity. P&E3

- Show particular interests. P&E4

- Pretend objects are things from their experience. P&E5

- Represent their experiences in play. P&E6

- Act out experiences with other people. P&E8

- Initiate activities. P&E9

- Seek challenge. P&E10

- Maintain focus on their activity for a period of time. AL1

- Show high levels of energy, fascination. AL2

- Persist with activity when challenges occur. AL5

- Show satisfaction in meeting their own goals. AL8

- Think of ideas. CTC1

- Plan, make decisions about how to approach a task, solve a problem and reach a goal. CTC8

## Positive relationships

(What adults could do)

Adults may:

- Play with children. Encourage them to explore, and show their own interest in discovering new things. P&E1

- Help children as needed to do what they are trying to do, without taking over or directing. P&E2

- Join in play sensitively, fitting in with children's ideas. P&E3

- Pay attention to how children engage in activities — the challenges faced, the effort, thought, learning and enjoyment. Talk more about the process than products. P&E6

- Support children to choose their activities – what they want to do and how they will do it. AL1

- Describe what they see children trying to do, and encourage children to talk about their own processes and successes. AL3

- Be specific when praising, especially noting effort such as how the child concentrates, tries different approaches, persists, solves problems, and has new ideas. AL4

- Use the language of thinking and learning: *think, know, remember, forget, idea, makes sense, plan, learn, find out, confused, figure out, trying to do.* CTC1

- Encourage open-ended thinking by not settling on the first ideas: *What else is possible?* CTC3

- Give children time to talk and think. CTC6

- Encourage children to describe problems they encounter, and to suggest ways to solve the problem. CTC11

## Enabling environments

(What adults could provide)

Adults could provide additional support by:

- Offering stimulating resources which are accessible and open-ended so they can be used, moved and combined in a variety of ways. P&E1

- Making sure resources are relevant to children's interests. P&E2

- Arranging flexible indoor and outdoor space and resources where children can explore, build, move and role play. P&E3

- Ensuring children have uninterrupted time to play and explore. P&E6

- Children will become more deeply involved when adults provide something that is new and unusual for them to explore, especially when it is linked to their interests. AL1

- Ensuring children have time and freedom to become deeply involved in activities. AL3

- Play is a key opportunity for children to think creatively and flexibly, solve problems and link ideas. Adults can promote the enabling conditions for rich play: space, time, flexible resources, choice, control, warm and supportive relationships. CTC3

- Plan linked experiences that follow the ideas children are really thinking about. CTC6

*Playing in the digging patch allows the children to engage in relationships with others.*

## Sand or mud kitchens

Sand and mud kitchens are a great place to delight the senses with fresh smelling herbs, water for mixing plus pebbles, leaves, flowers and pinecones to be used for 'cooking' ingredients.

The sand kitchen does not have to be separate from the sandpit, although if you have the room (or a spare sandpit) then why not. Otherwise, by using a dividing log, table or similar, you can create a separate space for a sand kitchen.

Pick sprigs of fresh rosemary and lavender or bring in carnations, roses or other flowers from home to use as 'ingredients' and decorative items in the sandpit. If you have an old home corner stove it can be used for 'cooking' sand cakes on.

## Large sand pits

It is important to spend time setting up the sandpit before the children arrive each day. Planning for play experiences in the sandpit should involve more than just putting out the buckets and spades.

Raking the sandpit before you set it up makes it look much fresher and more inviting. If the budget allows, have your sandpit topped up a couple of times a year so it has plenty of fresh sand in it. Ensuring you have a bucket per spade may reduce conflicts, although the sandpit is often great place to practise conflict resolution.

Children like to help, so rakes and brooms near the sandpit will encourage them to be responsible for their play environment.

Try to come up with new ideas for setting up the sandpit and rotate these ideas regularly to maintain interest and promote constructive play. Some ideas for the sandpit include large trucks, old plumbing pipes, buckets and spades, rocks, plenty of water, bamboo branches, leaves, artificial grass, witches' hats, construction signs, timber planks, tables, blocks, large dinosaurs or animals, wheelbarrows ... the list is endless.

Sometimes you may wish to set the sandpit up freshly clean and ordered. At other times it may have branches, rocks, hessian, plants and logs, and take on more of a rustic feel. Adding tall branches such as bamboo gives it a feeling of privacy and wonder.

Adding blocks, rocks, pipes and water opens up great opportunities for extending play and learning.

# Chapter 14

# Sensory experiences

Sensory experiences can have a calming effect on many children. Filling a bucket with water, letting warm sand fall between your fingers or toes or pushing your hands through slime, shaving cream or finger paint are all very relaxing play experiences.

On the other hand, some children don't like sensory experiences at all. These children may enjoy 'cleaner' sensory experiences like the seed, rice or playing at a sensory wall.

## Early Learning Goals from the EYFS

Playing with sensory materials and experiences enables children to work towards the following early learning goals. Key features of these related to sensory play are identified in italics:

### Personal, social and emotional development

Self-confidence and self-awareness:

*Children are confident to try new activities, and say why they like some activities more than others*. They are confident to speak in a familiar group, will talk about their ideas, and will choose the resources they need for their chosen activities. They say when they do or don't need help.

Making relationships:

*Children play co-operatively, taking turns with others*. They take account of one another's ideas about how to organise their activity. They show sensitivity to others' needs and feelings, and form positive relationships with adults and other children.

### Communication and language

Speaking:

*Children express themselves effectively,* showing awareness of listeners' needs. They use past, present and future forms accurately when talking about events that have happened or are to happen in the future. They develop their own narratives and explanations by connecting ideas or events

## Physical development

Moving and handling:

*Children show good control and co-ordination in large and small movements.* They move confidently in a range of ways, safely negotiating space. *They handle equipment and tools effectively, including pencils for writing.*

Health and self-care:

Children know the importance for good health of physical exercise, and a healthy diet, and talk about ways to keep healthy and safe. *They manage their own basic hygiene and personal needs successfully,* including dressing and going to the toilet independently.

## Understanding the world

People and communities:

Children talk about past and present events in their own lives and in the lives of family members. They know that other children don't always enjoy the same things, and are sensitive to this. They know about similarities and differences between themselves and others, and among families, communities and traditions.

The world:

*Children know about similarities and differences in relation to places, objects, materials* and living things. They talk about the features of their own immediate environment and how environments might vary from one another. They make observations of animals and plants and explain why some things occur, and *talk about changes.*

## Expressive arts and design

Exploring and using media and materials:

Children sing songs, make music and dance, and experiment with ways of changing them. *They safely use and explore a variety of materials,* tools and techniques, experimenting with colour, design, texture, form and function.

*Using vegetables to create monsters!*

# Characteristics of Effective Learning

When children are learning through play with sensory materials, adults will be able to observe some of the Characteristics of Effective Learning from the EYFS. In this section, the photos are accompanied by some of these 'CEL' statements:

*(Note: In the following text, P&E = Playing and Exploring; AL = Active Learning; CTC= Creating and Thinking Critically)*

## The unique child

(observing how a child is learning)

Children may:

● Show curiosity about objects, events and people. P&E1

● Use senses to explore the world around them. P&E2

● Engage in open-ended activity. P&E3

● Represent their experiences in play. P&E6

● Show a 'can do' attitude. P&E11

● Take a risk, engage in new experiences, and learning by trial and error. P&E12

● Maintain focus on their activity for a period of time. AL1

● Show high levels of energy, fascination. AL2

● Be not easily distracted. AL3

● Enjoy meeting challenges for their own sake rather than external rewards or praise. AL10

● Make predictions. CTC5

● Test their ideas. CTC6

## Positive relationships

(What adults could do)

Adults may:

- Play with children. Encourage them to explore, and show their own interest in discovering new things. P&E1

- Help children as needed to do what they are trying to do, without taking over or directing. P&E2

- Join in play sensitively, fitting in with children's ideas. P&E3

- Encourage children to try new activities and to judge risks for themselves. Be sure to support children's confidence with words and body language. P&E5

- Pay attention to how children engage in activities - the challenges faced, the effort, thought, learning and enjoyment. Talk more about the process than products. P&E6

- Support children to choose their activities – what they want to do and how they will do it. AL1

- Stimulate children's interest through shared attention, and calm over-stimulated children. AL2

- Be specific when praising, especially noting effort such as how the child concentrates, tries different approaches, persists, solves problems, and has new ideas. AL4

- Always respect children's efforts and ideas, so they feel safe to take a risk with a new idea. CTC4

- Support children's interests over time, reminding them of previous approaches and encouraging them to make connections between their experiences. CTC8

- Give feedback and help children to review their own progress and learning. Talk with children about what they are doing, how they plan to do it, what worked well and what they would change next time. CTC13

## Enabling environments

(What adults could provide)

Adults could provide additional support by:

- Offering stimulating resources which are accessible and open-ended so they can be used, moved and combined in a variety of ways. P&E1

- Making sure resources are relevant to children's interests. P&E2

- Arranging flexible indoor and outdoor space and resources where children can explore, build, move and role play. P&E3

- Helping children concentrate by limiting noise and making spaces visually calm and orderly. P&E4

- Planning first-hand experiences and challenges appropriate to the development of the children. P&E5

- Ensuring children have uninterrupted time to play and explore. P&E6

- Children will become more deeply involved when adults provide something that is new and unusual for them to explore, especially when it is linked to their interests. AL1

- Ensuring children have time and freedom to become deeply involved in activities. AL3

- Keeping significant activities out instead of routinely tidying them away. AL5

- Building in opportunities for children to play with materials before using them in planned tasks. CTC2

- Develop a learning community which focuses on how and not just what we are learning. CTC8

Sensory experiences are often particularly important when working with children with additional needs. Communicating about these experiences with parents will support the child's individual needs.

## Slime, seeds, rice and water beads

Using rice, seeds and slime allows children to explore different sensory experiences, get messy and enjoy feeling these items between their fingers. Exploring words such as 'gooey', 'mushy', 'soft', 'warm', 'cold' and 'spikey' are great ways of developing language and understanding of the world around us.

Adding props such as animals, cups, jugs, tubes, whisks and rocks will enhance these experiences.

Storing rice and seeds in plastic containers between uses prevents wasting food. Using food in play is occasionally a controversial topic, therefore please only do what you are comfortable with. Don't use food if there are cultural or economic reasons against it. Decisions must be made on an individual basis.

Rice can be coloured using food dye. If you want more than one colour, then divide the rice evenly and colour each portion separately, making sure you dry it thoroughly before storing it away. Add just enough water to the food dye to wet the grains as you stir them through (approx. 1 cup), then remove all excess water and dry.

Water beads can be purchased from art and craft suppliers. They are tiny non-toxic beads that, when added to water, absorb the water and expand. They have a slimy texture but leave your hands clean after use. Children can watch them grow and predict how big they will get. Once expanded they can enjoy the feel of them.

## Sensory wall

This sensory wall was created by staff as a gift for the children. Over a period of time we gathered many sensory items to put on the wall. We invited families to bring in old bits of china, beads, rocks, fabric, shells, carpet, brushes, and anything else safe and sensory they had at home.

During the holidays, staff worked together one day to create the wall. For many years now, the children have enjoyed feeling all the items on the wall, looking in mirrors, opening and closing things and enjoying the sensory qualities of the wall.

# Sensory box

This sensory box is fun and you can easily make your own. The children take it turns to put their hands through the red circles to feel a variety of items on the other side.

Try a similar technique for smelling experiences. Gather a number of small containers, and fill them with different smelling items such as vanilla, vinegar, chocolate essence, fish sauce – anything you can think of that is non-toxic and smells great or awful! Place the bowls behind the holes or flaps, out of sight. Have the camera ready to capture the facial expressions.

# Water

Adding washing-up liquid to the water trough makes an interesting new sensation. Add colour too, and use the warm water– all these elements add to the sensory experience for the child.

A trickle stream is a wonderful addition to the setting. This stream runs all year round, and with the addition of different plastic animals or occasionally some bubble mix it is always a busy play area. Children are taught that the water continually recycles and therefore should not be taken away in buckets. It's a great way to have water in the setting without water wastage.

This treasure trove of sensory experiences includes water, logs, rocks, shells, gemstones and crocodiles!

Water experiences indoors are important too. Teach children to wipe up water spills with a towel provided.

# Ice

Freezing animals in water overnight creates a wonderful sensory experience on a hot day. Let children use hammers to break the dinosaurs free. Remind them to take care when using hammers and supervise carefully.

# Mud

This sensory mud activity uses an old tyre and hessian for a natural play experience.

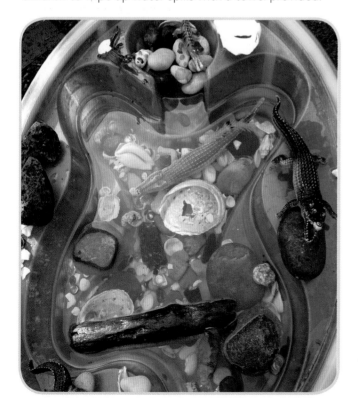

## Sensory science

Creating a compost bin not only teaches children about looking after their environment; it also allows them to play with dirt, straw, leaves and worms.

Adding food dye to water, and providing jugs, tubes, funnels and scoops creates a sensory activity that is also a maths and science experience.

Pom-poms are soft to touch and great for working out the volume of different containers.

# REFERENCES AND FURTHER READING

**Development Matters in the Early Years Foundation Stage**; early-education.org.uk/development matters

**Statutory Framework for the Early Years Foundation Stage**; www.foundationyears.org.uk/eyfs-statutory-framework

Helen Moylett, 2013, **Characteristics of Effective Learning** (OUP)

Nancy Stewart, 2011, **How Children Learn:** The Characteristics of Effective Learning, (The British Association for Early Childhood Education)

**Making a Mud Kitchen**; www.muddyfaces.co.uk/mud_kitchens.php

**Little Books** series; Various authors (Featherstone Education)

- Messy Play
- Clay and Malleable Materials
- Dough
- Explorations
- Investigations
- Fine Motor Skills
- Painting
- Sand and Water Play
- Treasure Boxes
- Tuff Spot Activitites

**50 Fantastic Things to do with…** series; Various authors (Featherstone Education)

- A sand tray
- A water tray
- Paint
- Squidgy stuff

**Making the Most of** series; Various authors (Featherstone Education)

- Light and Mirrors
- Reclaimed and Natural Materials
- Outdoor Learning